Guide to

IC11

Guide to

IC11

JCT Intermediate Building Contract (IC)

JCT Intermediate Building Contract with
Contractor's Design (ICD)

RIBA ⧓ **Publishing**

Sarah Lupton

Published by RIBA Publishing,
15 Bonhill Street, London EC2P 2EA

ISBN 978 1 85946 390 1

Stock code 74349

British Library Cataloguing in Publication Data
A catalogue record for this book is available from the British Library.

Commissioning Editor: James Thompson
Project Manager: Alasdair Deas
Typeset by: Academic + Technical Typesetting, Bristol
Printed and bound by: Charlesworth Group, Wakefield
Figures 14 and 15 by Rebecca Pike

RIBA Publishing is part of RIBA Enterprises Ltd.
www.ribaenterprises.com

Foreword

Developed historically for use with middle-range jobs, the 2011 edition of the Intermediate Building Contract is published in two versions – IC11 and ICD11 – to cater for the increasing importance of contractor's design. These contracts are intended for building works of simple content and without complex services installations, regardless of value or duration. The 2011 edition integrates changes in the Construction Act (in force from 1 October 2011), insurance and termination provisions and, amongst other things, reference to site waste management plans and the Bribery Act 2010.

Sarah Lupton's *Guide to IC11* covers all of these points and many more. It is a straightforward and comprehensive analysis of the form in the light of today's legal and practice landscape. Not only does she point out the important new changes, but she reflects on recent court cases which serve as valuable illustrations of the practical effects of the wording. The contract's provisions, procedures and supplementary conditions are spelled out authoritatively and are organised by theme. The hard-pressed practitioner familiar with the forms will be particularly pleased to see the useful indexes, and will doubtless come to depend on being able to dip quickly into the book for specific help during the course of a job.

I would also thoroughly recommend the book to both architecture and other construction students on the threshold of undertaking their professional examinations. The comprehensive up-to-date coverage clearly and succinctly exposes the legal ramifications of the contract. Sarah Lupton's rare combination of being a legally-trained architect who also runs the MA in Professional Studies at Cardiff University makes this book the ideal student companion.

Neil Gower, Solicitor
Chief Executive, The Joint Contracts Tribunal
September 2011

About the Author

Professor Sarah Lupton MA, DipArch, LLM, RIBA, CArb is a partner in Lupton Stellakis and directs the Diploma/MA in Professional Studies at the Welsh School of Architecture. She is dual qualified as an architect and as a lawyer. She lectures widely on subjects relating to construction law, is the author of many books on standard form building contracts, including this series, and is the co-editor (with Manos Stellakis) of a series on legislative controls. She contributes regularly to the *International Construction Law Review* and acts as an arbitrator, adjudicator and expert witness in construction disputes. She is an elected member of the Architects Registration Board and is currently head of its delegation to the Architects' Council of Europe. She is also vice-chair of the CIC's Liability Panel and a member of the RIBA President's Advisory Committee on Dispute Resolution.

Contents

About the Guide

The JCT Intermediate Form of Contract, although having a shorter history than the Standard Building Contract or the Minor Works form, is nevertheless an established industry benchmark and has become the first choice for many involved in medium to large-scale projects.

Publication of this third edition of the Guide was triggered by the revisions to the Housing Grants, Construction and Regeneration Act 1996, as effected by the Local Democracy, Economic Development and Construction Act 2009, which have resulted in significant revisions to payment clauses in the form. The third edition also covers other changes which have been introduced by the JCT since 2007, such as provisions covering agreed adjustments, collaborative working and environmental performance, and the 2011 edition of the form also incorporates new provisions on terrorism cover, as well as numerous minor adjustments to the clauses. Alongside these changes, as (for the first time) all four guides in the series were published together, the opportunity was taken to regularise the text and formatting across the series.

The Guide retains the structure and style of previous editions. It does not assume any prior knowledge of either IC11 or any previous editions of the form, and the subject is covered by topic, rather than by a clause-by-clause commentary. The Guide includes a broad outline of the form and the reasons why it might be selected. It describes the various documents that may form part of the contract package at the time it is entered into, and examines the contractor's obligations with respect to quality and standard of work, including the design obligations under ICD11. It also includes chapters on programming, control of the works, certification and payment, insurance, termination and dispute resolution. Brief introductions to legal concepts are included where necessary to understand the form's provisions. All court cases cited also include a short summary of the case, as it is felt that these examples help practitioners to understand the context of the legal point being made.

It is intended primarily for consultants such as architects or surveyors, who are advising clients on contracts and who may be acting as contract administrators, and also for students in the construction field. It will also be of use to lawyers who need an introduction to the form or a quick reminder of its key features.

The author would like to thank Rebecca Pike for her invaluable help in updating the series, both in reviewing the new forms to identify changes needed to the text and for redrafting many of the diagrams.

1   About IC11

1.1   The Intermediate Form of Building Contract is published in two versions. The first, referred to in this guide as IC11, is the equivalent of the original Intermediate Form of Contract, first published in 1984, and the second (ICD11) is a variant that incorporates provisions for contractor's design of part or parts of the works, similar to those that formed the basis of the Contractor's Designed Portion Supplement to JCT98. Except for the design provisions, both versions are identical, therefore although this guide generally refers to IC11, the points made will be applicable to both versions. The form is based on the same key rights and obligations that existed in IC05, and will therefore be familiar to users of that contract. IC11 and ICD11 are for use by both private clients and local authorities.

1.2   The Joint Contracts Tribunal (JCT) publishes several ancillary documents for use with IC11. These include a sub-contract agreement and conditions for use where a domestic sub-contractor is to carry out design (ICSub/D/A and ICSub/D/C) and one for use where it is not (ICSub/A and ICSub/C). A complete suite of forms is also published for use with named sub-contractors. This suite comprises a form of tender and agreement (ICSub/NAM) with three sections (an invitation to tender ICSub/NAM/IT, a tender form ICSub/NAM/T and an agreement ICSub/NAM/A), sub-contract conditions (ICSub/NAM/C) and a warranty for use between the employer and the named sub-contractor (ICSub/NAM/E). There is also an Intermediate Building Contract Guide (IC/G) and a Guide relating to the sub-contracts (ICSub/G). The JCT publishes collateral warranties to a funder (CWa/F) and purchaser or tenant (CWa/P&T) which may be used with IC11, as can the sub-contract collateral warranties to the same (SCWa/F and SCWa/P&T) and the sub-contractor warranty to the employer (SCWa/E). The JCT Adjudication Agreements, to be used when appointing an adjudicator, are also published separately.

Key features

1.3   IC11 is intended for use in a traditional procurement route context, where the contractor is required to carry out the work described briefly in the first recital and shown in the contract documents for the contract sum entered in Article 2, and to complete the work by the date or dates entered in the contract particulars. The contract makes reference throughout to an 'Architect/Contract Administrator' who is named in Article 3, and given various powers and duties under the contract, including the obligation to supply the contractor with all information reasonably necessary for carrying out the works (for simplicity, this Guide refers only to 'contract administrator' throughout). The contract contains provisions for varying the work, and adjusting the contract sum and the date for completion on the occurrence of certain events.

1.4   The quality and quantity of work to be carried out is that shown in the contract documents, therefore it is extremely important that the description of the works is accurate and comprehensive. The contract allows for a variety of combinations of contract documents, which may include drawings, a bill of quantities, specifications, schedules of work and schedules of rates. At tender stage the contractor prices either a bill of quantities, or specification, or schedule of works, or submits a contract sum analysis or schedule of rates as required.

1.5   ICD11 is also essentially a form for traditional procurement. However, it makes provision for the contractor to be required to design an identified part or parts of the works. If this version is selected, in addition to the documents mentioned above, the contractor will have been sent the employer's requirements for the project at the time of tender, and will have submitted its proposals for the design at tender stage. The employer's requirements and the contractor's proposals will form part of the contract documents. The contractor is also required to submit information regarding the developing design during the course of the project. ICD11, however, is not a design and build contract, and assumes that the majority of the project will be designed by the employer's consultants.

1.6   IC11 and ICD11 are both lump sum contracts, which means the works shown in the contract documents must be carried out for the contract sum 'or such other sum as shall become payable' under the contract (Article 2). Payment to the contractor is made at monthly intervals following the issue of contract administrator's certificates. In general terms, the certificates will reflect the amount of work that has been properly completed up to the point of valuation in accordance with the terms of the contract. All the requirements of the Housing Grants, Construction and Regeneration Act (HGCRA) 1996 Part II (as amended) regarding payment and notices are incorporated into IC11, and the provisions regarding contractor's price statements, contractor's applications for payment, listed items, activity schedules and advance payments, which were introduced into JCT98 alongside the 1996 Act's requirements, have also been stepped down into IC11.

1.7   As with other JCT traditional forms, the contractor may sub-contract the work to domestic sub-contractors with the written approval of the contract administrator. The key distinguishing feature of IC11, however, is the provisions allowing for the naming of sub-contractors, using the Intermediate Named Sub-Contract Tender & Agreement ICSub/NAM (note this does not apply to the execution of part of the works by a statutory undertaker acting in that capacity (Schedule 2:12)).

1.8   Under these provisions the contractor can be required to sub-contract to a specific contractor or supplier, who may be named either in the tender documents or, after the contract is let, in an instruction for the expenditure of a provisional sum. This allows the employer a great deal of flexibility and a high degree of control over who carries out the work and the terms on which it is done. The employer, however, takes some risk where, for example, the contractor may have the right to an extension of time for delays resulting from instructions relating to named sub-contractors (see Figure 1).

1.9   An additional flexibility is that the named sub-contractor provisions also allow for the sub-contractor to carry out design. If this is required it is essential that a direct warranty is arranged between the employer and the sub-contractor, as IC11 excludes any liability of the contractor for the design by named sub-contractors.

Figure 1 Distribution of risk associated with named sub-contractors

	Revision to contract sum?	Extension of time?	Loss and/or expense?
named sub-contractor's progress causes delay	no	no	no
delay in issuing instructions dealing with naming	no	yes (2·20·6)	yes (4·18·4)
compliance with instructions under Schedule 2 – paragraph 2	yes (3·11)	yes (2·20·2)	yes (4·18·2)
compliance with instructions under Schedule 2 – paragraph 5 (provisional sum)	yes (3·13)	yes (2·20·2)	yes (4·18·2)
following termination, compliance with instructions naming replacement sub-contractor under Schedule 2 – paragraph 7·1:			
if original sub-contractor named in contract documents Schedule 2 – paragraph 8·1	yes	yes (2·20·2)	no
if original sub-contractor named in instruction Schedule 2 – paragraph 9	yes	yes (2·20·2)	yes (4·18·2)
following termination, compliance with instructions under Schedule 2 – paragraphs 7·2 and 7·3	yes	yes (2·20·2)	yes (4·18·2)
following termination, where contractor has not complied with Schedule 2 – paragraph 6	reduction only	no	no

1.10   The named sub-contractor provisions are also included in ICD11 but, as indicated by a footnote in the contract, if the named sub-contractor has design responsibilities, the naming procedure should only be used for discrete parts of the works where the named sub-contractor is solely responsible for design. The naming provisions should not be used for any element of the works within the part or parts for which the contractor has design responsibility. Essentially, a named sub-contractor should not be required to carry out work within the contractor's designed portion. This is because of the conflict that will arise regarding design liability, as the main contractor would be simultaneously liable for such work under the designed portion provisions, but exempt from liability under the named sub-contract provisions.

1.11   In theory, a named sub-contractor could be required to carry out work which forms part of the contractor's designed portion in cases where the named sub-contractor is not to take on any design liability, but is merely to construct work designed by the contractor. In practice, though, the boundaries may not be that clear, and it may be best to avoid naming sub-contractors for any part of the designed portion work.

Deciding on IC11

1.12   The introduction to the Intermediate Building Contract Guide (IC/G) (and the inside front cover of the form) state that IC11 is primarily intended for use:

- 'where the proposed building works are of simple content involving the normal, recognised basic trades and skills of the industry, without building service installations of a complex nature or other complex specialist work;

- where the works are designed by or on behalf of the Employer, fairly detailed contract provisions are necessary and the Employer is to provide the Contractor with drawings and bills of quantities, a specification or work schedules to define adequately the quantity and quality of the work; and

- where an Architect/Contract Administrator and Quantity Surveyor are to administer the conditions.'

1.13   In practice, IC11 is suitable for a very wide range of project types and sizes. The JCT no longer suggests financial limits on where it might be appropriate to use the form, and it would be suitable for a wide range of contract values. There are, however, some situations where the form would not be suitable. Care should be taken where the client is a consumer, particularly where carrying out work to a dwelling which the client intends to occupy. The HGCRA 1996 Part II does not apply in this situation, and some of the 1998 revisions may be considered unfair under the Unfair Terms in Consumer Contracts Regulations 1999 (SI 1999/2083), if not individually negotiated with the client prior to entering into the contract (*Domsalla* v *Dyason*). The contract may also be unsuitable where the quantity or type of work is largely unknown, or where the work is extremely complex.

Domsalla v *Dyason* [2007] BLR 348

The employer, Mr Dyason, whose house had burnt down, was advised by his insurers to enter into a contract based on MW98 with the contractor, Domsalla. The employer saw the form for the first time at the first site meeting, when he was presented with it for signature. The project was delayed, and the employer did not pay the sums certified in the last three certificates for payment, totalling £127,871.33, but no withholding notices were served. The contractor initiated an adjudication and the adjudicator decided in its favour against the owner. Subsequently, the Technology and Construction Court refused to enforce the decision and the employer was given leave to defend the claim on the ground that the withholding notice provisions of the contract were unfair under the Unfair Terms in Consumer Contracts Regulations 1999, and were therefore not binding on him as a consumer.

1.14   Where the contractor is to design discrete part(s) of the works, even though all the other criteria are met, the parties should use the Intermediate Building Contract with Contractor's Design (ICD11). The Guide makes it clear that this form is not, however, to be used for a 'design and build' procurement route, where a form such as the JCT DB11 would be more suitable.

Figure 2 Comparison with SBC11 and MWD11

Comparison with SBC11	**Comparison with MWD11**
• Version without contractor design.	• More extensive design provisions.
• Provisions for named sub-contractors.	• Professional indemnity insurance clause.
• No Schedule 2 quotations.	• Provisions for named sub-contractors.
• Only one fluctuations option.	• More detailed requirements for sub-contracts.
• No CDP design submission procedure.	• Ability to defer possession.
• No third party rights.	• Partial possession and sectional completion
• Default retention deduction is 5 per cent, not	provisions.
3 per cent.	• Collateral warranties may be required.

1.15   The provisions for naming of sub-contractors may be particularly useful where design is required by known specialist firms. This is a common requirement in practice with specialist design items such as mechanical services or prefabricated elements. Under this arrangement it is possible for the employer to enter into a warranty with the specialist (ICSub/NAM/E) at an early stage, so that the design can be integrated into the project as a whole, with the safeguard to the specialist that, if it is not awarded the sub-contract, it will be paid for any design work carried out. Even where design is not an issue, there may be circumstances in which the employer wishes part of the work to be carried out by a particular firm.

1.16   There are, however, some risks to the employer in naming sub-contractors, although these are not so extensive as had been the case with the nominated sub-contractor provisions in JCT98. Generally, the contractor takes full responsibility for the performance of named sub-contractors, including for their progress on site, except that delays in the naming process, such as in issuing instructions naming the sub-contractor, would be the employer's risk, as would delays resulting from a termination of the sub-contract due to the sub-contractor's default. The main contractor is also entirely responsible for payment – there is no requirement to name amounts due to named sub-contractors in certificates, nor any obligation on the employer to pay the sub-contractor direct should the contractor fail to do so. In addition, the procedures associated with naming the sub-contractor are slightly simpler than those for nomination, although they are still by no means straightforward. On balance, the naming provisions have proved popular with construction professionals, and are often one of the main reasons for selecting this form.

1.17   The form is laid out under 'section headed' format, which by and large groups the clauses in a logical fashion. The 2005 version had streamlined much of the drafting and removed some of the overly complex passages that were problematic in the 1998 version and had seemed out of proportion to the form as a whole. Overall, it is a simpler document than SBC11 for relatively straightforward projects of the scale envisaged, and avoids many of the gaps and pitfalls of MW11 (see Figure 2). It is therefore a popular choice for medium to large-scale projects.

Pre-2011 revisions to the 2005 edition

1.18   Prior to the new 2011 edition, the JCT had published three sets of adjustments to the 2005 terms: Amendment 1 (April 2007), relating to the CDM Regulations 2007; Revision 1 (June 2007), comprising various updates and corrections; and a new form of attestation

(February 2008). All of these were subsequently incorporated into Revision 2, published in 2009. Revision 2 primarily dealt with three particular aims: to introduce new 'sustainable development' requirements; to reflect the criteria set out in the Office of Government Commerce's Achieving Excellence in Construction initiative (thereby removing the remaining barriers to the adoption of JCT contracts across all central government departments); and to modify the payment provisions. The 2009 Revision 2 changes can be summarised as follows:

- reference to a 'Framework Agreement' added (ninth recital, or twelfth in ICD05);

- general requirement for all communications to be in writing (avoids repeating 'in writing' throughout the form) (cl 1·7·1);

- option for parties to agree means of communication (e.g. by email), with exceptions in some cases (such as notices of termination) (cl 1·7·2);

- new requirement for the contractor to use JCT forms of sub-contract 'where considered appropriate' (cl 3·6);

- requirement on both parties to work collaboratively (new Supplemental Provision 1);

- best practice health and safety requirement (new Supplemental Provision 2);

- contractor encouraged to propose cost savings and value improvements (new Supplemental Provision 3);

- contractor encouraged to propose amendments to improve environmental performance (new Supplemental Provision 4);

- option to include performance indicators (new Supplemental Provision 5);

- notification for early warning of disputes followed by negotiation (new Supplemental Provision 6);

- requirement that both parties give serious consideration to any request by the other to enter mediation (cl 9·1).

Changes in the 2011 edition

1.19   The key reason for bringing out the 2011 editions of the JCT forms was the changes necessitated by the revisions to the HGCRA 1996, which were brought in by the Local Democracy, Economic Development and Construction Act (LDEDCA) 2009. Other changes introduced by the JCT include revisions to insurance provisions and a new definition of insolvency. The main changes in the 2011 edition of IC are listed in Figure 3.

IC11 changes due to the LDEDCA 2009

1.20   The LDEDCA 2009 came into force on 1 October 2011, together with a revised Scheme for Construction Contracts, which, as before, acts as a fallback set of provisions if parties

Figure 3 Key changes

Clause	Revised/new	Key changes
Article 6	revised	Principal contractor role extended to include that under the Site Waste Management Plans Regulations 2008
Contract particulars	revised	References to dates of interim certificates changed to 'due dates' (cl 4·7·1)
Contract particulars	revised	Terrorism cover added (cl 6·10)
Contract particulars (ICD only)	revised	Entries in respect of professional indemnity insurance relating to asbestos and fungal mould have been removed (cl 6·16)
Contract particulars	revised	List of adjudicator nominating bodies changed (cl 9·2·1)
1·1	revised	'Final Payment Notice', 'Interim Application', 'Interim Payment Notice', 'Pay Less Notice', 'SWMP Regulations' added to defined terms
4·7·1	revised	Due dates to be either at monthly intervals or at specified dates
4·7·2	revised	Certificates to be issued within 5 days of due dates
4·10·1	revised	The contractor may make interim applications not less than seven days before the due date, setting out the amount it considers is due and the basis on which that sum is calculated (replaces the previous cl 4·6·3)
4·10·2	new	When no interim certificate is issued, the contractor may issue an interim payment notice within five days of the due date (if an interim payment application has been made, this has the same effect as an interim payment notice)
4·11·5	revised	The employer issues a 'Pay Less Notice' when it considers a sum other than the sum stated as due (that is, the sum in the certificate or if not issued the interim application) is due
4·12·1	revised	The pay less notice appears to be wider in scope than the withholding notice, as it deals with value as well as deductions or counterclaims
4·12·2	new	A payment notice and a pay less notice have to be issued even where the sum due is zero
4·13.2	new	Costs due to suspension dealt with under separate clause
4·14·1	revised	Timing of due date for final payment adjusted
4·14·4	new	The employer or contractor may issue a pay less notice in relation to the final certificate (i.e. whichever party is the payer may give notice that it intends to pay less than the certified amount)
4·14·6	revised	In the absence of a final certificate, the contractor may issue a payment notice stating the amount it considers due and the basis on which the amount was calculated
6·8	revised	Definition of 'Pool Re Cover' added
6·10	new	Extension of policy to include terrorism cover
8·1	revised	New definition of insolvency
8·7·3 and 8·12·1	new	If a contractor becomes insolvent after the date for issuing a pay less notice has expired, the employer need not make payment

do not include clauses complying with the HGCRA 1996 in their own contracts. The changes are outlined below and summarised in Figure 3.

Scope and application of the HGCRA 1996

1.21   So far as construction is concerned, the HGCRA 1996 relates to payment provisions and to dispute resolution (adjudication) and the recent changes have not extended its scope to other areas. However, its application is extended somewhat. Under the HGCRA 1996 it was a requirement that, in order for it to apply to a construction contract, the contract had to be an agreement in writing. Under the LDEDCA changes this is no longer the case and the revised HGCRA applies to oral or part-oral contracts (section 107 is repealed). The new Act does, however, require the contract to include a provision 'in writing' as to the right to adjudicate and a requirement for the adjudicator to reach a decision (section 108, as amended). These changes will not normally affect the users of JCT forms, which would be 'in writing'. Section 109(1)(a) in the HGCRA 1996, which limits the Act's payment regime to contracts where the works take 45 days or longer, has not been amended by the new Act.

Notices

1.22   The LDEDCA 2009 introduced new payment provisions, which in summary give both employer and contractor (payer and payee) the right to issue payment notices. The overall effect is to tighten up the certification and payments system to further protect the contractor's right to be paid any amounts due.

1.23   Under the revised HGCRA 1996, the contract must require the payer or a 'specified person' to give a payment notice to the payee specifying the sum due and the 'basis on which that sum is calculated' not later than five days after the payment due date (section 110A(1)(a)). Alternatively, it may require the payee to give a payment notice to the payer specifying the sum that the payee considers to be due and the basis on which it is calculated not later than five days after the payment due date (section 109(1)(b)). The introduction of the 'specified person' as an alternative to the 'payer' means that the contract administrator may issue the notices on behalf of the employer. In IC11 the first notice is aligned with the payment certificate. Key changes since the 2005 edition are therefore: (1) the removal of the employer's first notice of payment and its replacement with the certificate itself, and (2) the timing of the certificates: the 'due dates' are entered into the contract particulars (not the dates of the certificates) and the certificates must be issued within five days of the due dates. As the final date for payment is 14 days after the due date, the effect is that, if the certifier waits the full five days allowed before issuing a certificate, the time available for payment will be reduced to nine days.

1.24   The Act then states that the payer or specified person may give a notice of its intention to pay less than the notified sum. The 'Pay Less Notice' must specify the sum that the payer considers to be due on the date the notice is served and the basis on which that sum is calculated (section 111(2)). It must be given not later than the period prescribed in the contract for the giving of such a notice or, if a period is not set out in the contract, a period that is not later than seven days before the final date for payment. The pay less notice therefore follows a similar procedure as the 'withholding notice' did in the 2005 form. The

JCT has retained the requirement that the employer and not a specified person should issue this notice.

1.25   More significantly, the Act now requires that, if the payer or specified person fails to give a payment notice as required under the contract, the payee may give a payment notice to the payer at any time after the payer's notice was due (section 110B). This means that if the contract administrator fails to issue a certificate, the contractor could issue a payment notice at any time prior to the final date for payment. If the payee gives such a notice, the final date for payment is postponed by the same number of days after the payment due date that the notice was given (section 110B(3)).

1.26   The payer is required to pay the notified sum on or before the final date for payment (section 111(1)). The 'notified sum' could be the amount in the payer's or the payee's notice, as the case may be (section 111(2)). All these requirements have been transposed into the IC11 form; therefore, if the contractor has made an application for payment and no certificate or notice is issued, this will become the amount payable. Where no application is made but no certificate is issued, the contractor may issue a payment notice and, subject to any pay less notice issued by the employer, this will become the amount due.

1.27   The Act provides that section 111(10) (the duty to pay the notified sum) does not apply where (1) the contract provides that, if the payee becomes insolvent the payer need not pay any sum due in respect of the payment, and (2) the payee has become insolvent after the prescribed period referred to in section 111(5)(a). This reflects the situation that was the subject of litigation in *Melville Dundas* v *Wimpey* (see paragraph 9.19).

Suspension

1.28   JCT clauses had treated the exercise of the right to suspension as a relevant event in relation to extensions of time and a relevant matter for the purposes of a loss and/or expenses claim, even though the 1996 Act said nothing about the consequences of suspension except that a payee was entitled to an extension of time for the period that the carrying out of the works is suspended for non-payment. The LDEDCA 2009 extends the payee's rights so that the payee is also entitled to an extension for any additional period for restarting the works after a period of suspension, and to the 'reasonable costs and expenses' of suspension and recommencement. The former would have been the case in any event under IC05, therefore no change was needed; however, the JCT has moved the claim of costs from the loss/expense section to a clause of its own (cl 4·13·2), probably so that the provision can more exactly follow the wording as set out in the Act.

Banning of 'pay when certified' clauses

1.29   The HGCRA 1996 stipulated that any clauses making payment conditional on having been paid are ineffective, but the LDEDCA 2009 widens the scope so that the ban now includes 'pay when certified' clauses, and also any requirement regarding the performance of obligations under another contract or a decision by any person as to whether obligations under another contract have been performed. None of the JCT standard sub-contracts have ever included such provisions.

Adjudication

1.30   The 2009 Act also bans what are termed 'Tolent clauses', which are essentially clauses whereby the parties agree that one party will pay the whole cost of the adjudication, regardless of the outcome. The JCT forms do not include details as to adjudication, as they rely on the default provisions in the Scheme for Construction Contracts, which do not include such a clause.

2 Documents

2.1 Documents are a key factor in the success of every building project and traditional projects, such as those under IC11 (or ICD11), depend on comprehensive and accurate information at tender stage. Ideally, the formal contract documents should be executed before the project commences on site. Normally, a contract is formed if there is a clear acceptance of a firm offer (see Peter Aeberli, *Focus on Construction Contract Formation*, RIBA Publishing, 2003). The contract, once executed, will supersede any conflicting provisions in the accepted tender and will apply retrospectively (*Tameside Metropolitan BC* v *Barlow Securities*). Any supplementary information should be provided in adequate time and to an agreed and workable programme. Inadequate and late information is very likely to result in an escalating budget and delays to the completion date.

Tameside Metropolitan Borough Council v *Barlow Securities Group Services Limited* [2001] BLR 113

Under JCT63 Local Authorities, Barlow Securities was contracted to build 106 houses for Tameside. A revised tender was submitted in September 1982 and work started in October 1982. By the time the contract was executed, 80 per cent of building work had been completed, and two certificates of practical completion were issued relating to seven of the houses in December 1983 and January 1994. Practical completion of the last houses was certified in October 1984. The retention was released under an interim certificate in October 1987. Barlow Securities did not submit any final account, although at a meeting in 1988 the final account was discussed. Defects appeared in 1995 and Tameside issued a writ on 9 February 1996. It was agreed between the parties that a binding agreement had been reached before work had started, and the only difference between the agreement and the executed contract was that the contract was under seal. It was found that there was no clear and unequivocal representation by Tameside that it would not rely on its rights in respect of defects. Time began to run in respect of the defects from the dates of practical completion; the first seven houses were therefore time barred. Tameside was not prevented from bringing the claim by failure to issue a final certificate.

2.2 When using IC11, the primary document is, of course, the printed form itself, which comprises not only articles and conditions but also various schedules, including forms of bonds and fluctuations provisions (see Figure 4). IC11 also makes reference to various other documents, not all of which are termed 'Contract Documents'. These other documents may nevertheless be included in the tender documents, or form part of the contract by incorporation by reference, or in some other way be of contractual effect. The recitals refer to drawings, bills of quantities, specification, works schedules, ICSub/NAM, a contract sum analysis, a schedule of rates, a priced activity schedule and an information release schedule. In addition, ICD11 refers to employer's requirements and contractor's proposals. The conditions refer to numerous further documents including, for example, the construction phase plan and the Joint Fire Code. Figure 5 indicates some of the possible combinations of documents that may make up the contract package for IC11.

Figure 4 Layout of the form

Articles of Agreement:
Recitals
Articles
Contract Particulars
Attestation

Conditions:
Section 1: Definitions and Interpretation
Section 2: Carrying out the Works
Section 3: Control of the Works
Section 4: Payment
Section 5: Variations
Section 6: Injury, Damage and Insurance
Section 7: Assignment and Collateral Warranties
Section 8: Termination
Section 9: Settlement of Disputes

Schedules:
Schedule 1: Insurance Options
Schedule 2: Named Sub-Contractors
Schedule 3: Forms of Bonds
Schedule 4: Fluctuations Option
Schedule 5: Supplemental Provisions

Figure 5 Possible combinations of documents

	Pricing Option A	**Pricing Option B**
Drawings	CD	CD
Employer's requirements	CD (ICD11 only)	CD (ICD11 only)
Contractor's proposals	CD (ICD11 only)	CD (ICD11 only)
CDP analysis	CD (ICD11 only)	CD (ICD11 only)
Priced bill of quantities/specification/work schedules (the priced document)	CD	
Specification (unpriced)		CD
Contract sum analysis/schedule of rates (the priced document)		R
Priced activity schedule	R	R
Information release schedule	R	R
Construction phase plan	cl 3·18·2	cl 3·18·2

KEY
CD = a 'Contract Document'
R = referred to in the recitals
cl = referred to in the conditions

Contract documents

2.3   The 'Contract Documents' are defined under clause 1·1, which sets out two alternatives. Both include the agreement and the conditions (found in the form), and the contract drawings together with, in the case of ICD11, the employer's requirements, the contractor's proposals and the CDP analysis. Both also include, if relevant, particulars of the Intermediate Named Sub-Contract and Agreement, with ICSub/NAM/IT and ICSub/NAM/T completed, for all sub-contractors named in the contract documents (see paragraph 2.28). In addition, under Pricing Option A the contract documents will include either a priced specification, or priced work schedules or a priced bill of quantities, referred to as the 'Priced Document'. Under Pricing Option B the contract documents will include an unpriced specification (fourth recital, or fifth in ICD11).

2.4   The essential difference between the two pricing options is that in Option A the contractor is given the document to be priced (specification, bills or schedules), which subsequently becomes a contract document, whereas with Option B the contractor simply states a sum and provides a breakdown in the form of a contract sum analysis, or provides a schedule of rates. This document is referred to as the 'Priced Document' but is not termed a 'Contract Document'. (IC/G explains that under Option B this is not a document that describes the works, and hence it is not defined as a contract document.) A priced activity schedule can be used with either option but is also not termed a 'Contract Document'. It should be noted, however, that, if used, the contract sum analysis, schedule of rates or activity schedule will have a contractual effect.

2.5   The articles of agreement must be completed very carefully (for guidance on completing the form see David Chappell, *IC11 Contract Administration Guide*, RIBA Publishing, 2011). The contract particulars require selection between alternative options, and insertion of data specific to the project, all of which must be completed carefully and accurately. The articles of agreement also contain the attestation that must be signed by both parties and witnessed, and special procedural steps must be taken if the contract is to be executed as a deed.

Contract drawings

2.6   The 'Contract Drawings' are listed under the second recital (or third in ICD11). These should all be identified precisely, including revision numbers, etc. The list may be annexed if long, but if so the list must be clearly identified. Note that in IC11 there is no reference to the party responsible for preparing the drawings. The contract requires that the parties sign all the drawings. For good practice in preparation and co-ordination of specification, drawings and bills of quantities, see current relevant publications on by the Construction Project Information Committee (CPIC).

The priced document

2.7   The fourth recital (or fifth in ICD11) Pricing Option A refers to the contractor having 'priced the Bills of Quantities/Specification/Work Schedules'. Two of these should be deleted as appropriate, and the total figure shown on the 'Priced Document' should be the contract sum as entered in Article 2. Bills of quantities would normally be used on larger or more complex projects, and would be prepared by the quantity surveyor according to the rules in the Standard Method of Measurement 7th edition (SMM7) (cl 2·12·1). Bills are particularly helpful when it comes to the accurate comparison of tender figures and valuation of variations. Schedules of work are often a useful alternative for smaller projects and can be arranged in any appropriate format. This is frequently by work sections or by trade, although a room-by-room basis is sometimes used in refurbishment projects. Drawings plus specification alone would normally only be used on simple projects where few variations are anticipated. Whichever document is used, it should be noted that, if materials or goods are to be paid for prior to delivery on site, a list of these must be annexed (cl 4·9).

2.8   Even where either bills or schedules of work are used, a specification would normally be prepared by the contract administrator, and in some cases all three types of document may form part of the project information. If the specification and/or schedules are to form part of the tender package alongside the bills, it is best to organise these as one document, i.e. as numbered sections of the bills. Alternatively, a schedule may form one of the numbered drawings. If a document sent out to tender is not referred to accurately in the first recital, there could be room for doubt later as to whether it forms part of the binding agreement between the parties.

2.9   The fourth recital (fifth in ICD11) Pricing Option B refers to the contractor having stated the sum it will require for carrying out the works (the 'Contract Sum' entered in Article 2) and provided a contract sum analysis or schedule of rates. The contract sum analysis could be in any form required, e.g. the contractor could even be asked to prepare a full bill of quantities, although this would be unlikely on smaller projects. A schedule of rates on its own is unlikely to be a very useful document. It is important to note that, although the contract sum analysis is not a contract document, it becomes a 'Priced Document' for the purposes of clause 5·3 (valuing of variations) and to that extent the employer is bound by its terms. As the document will be used for preparing valuations and assessing the value of variations, it would be wise to set out what format would be acceptable in the tender documents.

Activity schedule

2.10   The fourth recital (fifth in ICD11) also refers to a priced activity schedule, which is required under both Option A and Option B. If an activity schedule is not required, the provision must be deleted (Footnote 6, or 7 in ICD11). The activity schedule is defined in the fourth recital (fifth in ICD11) as a 'schedule of activities', which should be attached to the form. The schedule is prepared and priced by the contractor and provided prior to the contract being executed. An example of a priced activity schedule was included in the guidance notes to JCT80 Amendment 18, and it is very similar to a schedule of work. Each activity is priced, and the sum of those prices must equal the contract sum, with certain exclusions, namely provisional and prime cost sums and related contractor's profit, and the value of work for which approximate quantities have been included in the contract documents.

2.11   This is a rather curious provision to find in the form, where it is already anticipated that there will be a priced document which, with the possible exception of the priced specification under Option A and the schedule of rates under Option B, is likely to have the price broken down in considerable detail. The function of the activity schedule is to ascertain the value of work properly executed for certification purposes and, if included, the breakdown on the activity schedule will be used rather than that given in any other priced document. It will certainly give clear information as to how much value the contractor attaches to each activity and ensure that the certificates reflect this. However, it would be possible for contractors to 'front load' the activity schedule in order to improve their cash flow in the early stages, as there is no obligation for the schedule to reflect the prices given in the bills. Where it is to be used, the contract administrator should therefore be alert to any potential problems of this sort, which should be dealt with at tender stage before the contract is formed. It should be noted that, even if an activity schedule is used, the priced document will remain the basis for the valuation of variations.

Employer's requirements (ICD11 only)

2.12   The 'Employer's Requirements' are referred to in the fourth recital of ICD11 as 'documents showing or describing or otherwise stating his requirements for the design and construction of the Contractor's Designed Portion', and the form assumes that these have been sent to the contractor at tender stage.

2.13   The contract does not stipulate any format for the employer's requirements. In broad terms, the documents will set out the employer's requirements for the contractor's designed portion of the works. The requirements should be prepared carefully and on the assumption that there will be no changes to the requirements once the contract is let, for although the contract contains provisions whereby a variation can be instructed, such variations may result in additional costs to the employer and are subject to the consent of the contractor.

2.14   The requirements could be in a very summary format; for example, simply giving a brief description of the relevant part or system, with reference to drawings indicating its location and co-ordinating dimensions. It is likely, though, that they will be more detailed than that and will include a detailed specification, in either prescriptive or performance terms or, in all probability, involving a mixture of the two. They could also include schematic layouts or outline designs of the relevant part. In essence, they act as a brief. Advice on briefing is outside the scope of this Guide but reference could be made, for example, to David Hyams, *Construction Companion to Briefing*, RIBA Publications (2001). Consultants may also find the *JCT Guide to the Use of Performance Specifications*, RIBA Publications (2001) helpful when preparing the requirements.

2.15   One of the most important inclusions is to stipulate in exactly what form the proposals should be submitted and what they should include. This is essential in order for the employer to make a clear assessment of the submitted tenders. The amount and level of detail of the information will depend on the scale of the designed portion and its relationship with the rest of the design. Where the contractor's designed portion forms a significant element in the project, full information may be needed in order to integrate this element with other elements of the design, and in such cases the employer may need to adopt a two-stage tender approach.

2.16   It is also very important that the requirements should specify the drawings and other design information (the 'Contractor's Design Documents') to be submitted by the contractor following acceptance of tender, and a programme for their submission. The purpose of this is to control the scope, format and timing of the submission of design documents for review. For example, it should protect the contract administrator from being overwhelmed by design documents at an inconvenient time, or from being presented with design documents to review for key elements in isolation from information on other related aspects of the design. It is likely that the programme will be the subject of negotiation at tender, as it is important that any programme in the requirements will also meet the contractor's needs in terms of developing the design at a rate which will support its intended construction programme. It would also be wise to set out the information required to be submitted at practical completion, such as 'as built drawings', otherwise the contractor's obligation is to provide such information 'as the Employer may reasonably require' (cl 2·32).

Contractor's proposals (ICD11 only)

2.17   The contractor's proposals are normally submitted with the contractor's tender (sixth recital) and should be in the format and contain the information stipulated in the employer's requirements. These may request that various documents are provided, including drawings, specifications, schedules, programmes, method statements, etc.

2.18   The contractor should raise matters relating to the contract data where decisions are outstanding from the employer, so that these can be resolved. The proposals should indicate clearly any areas of conflict in the requirements, and any instances where the contractor has found it necessary to amend or amplify the brief. The contract does not allow for the inclusion of provisional sums in the proposals, only in the requirements, so if the contractor wishes to cover any part of the proposals with a provisional sum then it should inform the employer so that the requirements can be amended.

CDP analysis (ICD11 only)

2.19   The contract does not prescribe a format for the CDP analysis. It would therefore be sensible to set out what format would be acceptable in the employer's requirements. (It would not be unreasonable, in cases where the designed portion forms a significant part of the works, for the contractor to be asked to prepare a full bill of quantities, although this would be unlikely on smaller projects.) The contract requires that the document is used for assessing the value of employer-instructed variations to the contractor's designed portion (cl 5·7·2). It does not require that the document is used to assess the value of work carried out, etc., to be included in periodic payments, but it would normally be used by the contractor to prepare applications for payment, and by the employer in checking such applications.

Information release schedule

2.20   The 'Information Release Schedule' is referred to in the sixth recital (ninth in ICD11). It is an optional provision (the recital is deleted if the schedule is not provided). The schedule should state what 'information the Architect/Contract Administrator will release and the time of that release'. If used, the schedule is prepared by the contract administrator and sent out with the tender documents. The schedule does not need to list all the information that will be provided, but could, for example, list key drawings.

2.21 If the information release schedule is used, then the information shown in it must be supplied at the dates indicated (cl 2·10). With respect to information not shown on the schedule, or where a schedule is not used, the contract administrator is under an obligation to provide 'such further drawings or details as are reasonably necessary' (cl 2·11·1) either in sufficient time to allow the contractor to complete by the date for completion, or, if the contractor appears unlikely to complete by this date, at a date when 'having regard to the progress of the Works' it is reasonably necessary for the contractor to receive the information (cl 2·11·2). Failure to provide the information may constitute a ground for an extension of time (cl 2·20·6) and a 'Relevant Matter' which may give rise to a direct loss and/or expense claim (cl 4·18·4).

2.22 The advantage of using the information release schedule is that it gives the contract administrator the opportunity to prepare a realistic programme of drawing production, so that the contractor has a clear picture regarding information provision before submitting a tender. The contractor will not be able subsequently to request information by dates earlier than those shown; thus, the schedule will prevent the manoeuvring which sometimes occurs where lists of information are requested at the start of a project in the hope of setting the scene for a later claim. Used carefully, the information release schedule can therefore be a very effective management tool, provided the programme set out does not contain too much 'wishful thinking' on the part of the consultant team! If the contractor feels the schedule is awkward in terms of its planned operations, then adjustment could be negotiated at tender stage. The contract contains no provisions allowing the contract administrator unilaterally to adjust the programme, for example where an extension of time is granted or the contractor is running behind programme. As it would be to both parties' advantage for the document to remain a realistic representation of when information is required, it may be sensible to make allowance in the tender documents for updates to be negotiated, perhaps at monthly progress meetings.

Health and safety documents

2.23 Clauses 3·18 and 3·19 will be applicable where the contract particulars indicate that the project is notifiable under the Construction (Design and Management) Regulations (CDM) 2007 (entry relating to the seventh or tenth recitals), and this will usually be the case with IC11. The clauses specifically refer to the 'Construction Phase Plan' and the 'health and safety file'.

2.24 The construction phase plan is not a contract document under IC11, and the recitals make no mention of it having been prepared and given to the contractor at the time of tender. Nevertheless, it is a statutory obligation for the employer to ensure that a construction phase plan is prepared before construction work begins (Regulation 16). The employer must provide the contractor with pre-construction information, which is usually sent out with the tender documents. Before construction work can begin, the contractor must have developed the plan to comply with Regulation 23(a). To avoid uncertainty, it is advisable to require that this document is submitted well in advance of the date of possession. It should be noted that the contract requires that a pre-construction 'CDM Planning Period' is identified in the contract particulars, to allow time for planning and preparation in accordance with Regulation 10(2)(c).

2.25   The health and safety file is principally a matter for the CDM co-ordinator, who will compile it, but there is a requirement on the contractor to provide information for this file and to ensure that any sub-contractor also complies. The contract administrator, when certifying practical completion, must make sure that the contractor has 'complied sufficiently' with this requirement before issuing the certificate (cl 2·21).

Bonds

2.26   IC11 refers to two bonds: an advance payment bond and a bond in respect of payment for off-site materials and/or goods (note the provisions for advance payments do not apply where the employer is a local authority). Where required, the contractor must arrange bonds and, as both are optional, it must be made clear to the contractor at tender stage if either will be required. The former is normally required where an advance payment is to be made to the contractor under clause 4·6, and the latter where it has been agreed that certain materials or goods will be paid for prior to them being brought on site (cl 4·8·1·3 and 4·9). Terms for each of the bonds have been agreed between the British Bankers Association and JCT Ltd and are included in the form in Schedule 3 Parts 1 and 2. If any other terms are preferred, or if any other type of bond is required, such as a performance bond, then this must be made clear at tender stage, and the terms should be given to the contractor before the contract is entered into. In practice, the alternative terms should be sent out with the tender documents, so that the contractor can include them in the tender figure. If the contractor proposes alternative terms, then these should be forwarded to the client for discussion with the client's lawyers. Contract administrators do not normally have sufficient knowledge to advise the client on the terms of bonds.

Domestic sub-contracts

2.27   JCT Ltd publishes two versions of a standard form for use with IC11 domestic sub-contracts, one for use where a design obligation is to be sub-contracted, and one where it is not (the Agreements ICSub/A and ICSub/D/A, and Conditions ICSub/C and ICSub/D/C). There is no requirement under IC11 that the main contractor should use this form; however, there are restrictions on the terms that may be agreed. These are set out in clause 3·6·2 of IC11, which requires that particular conditions relating to ownership of unfixed goods and materials, and the right to interest on unpaid amounts properly due to the sub-contractor, are included in all domestic sub-contracts. The sub-contract should also, of course, comply with the requirements of the Housing Grants, Construction and Regeneration Act (HGCRA) 1996 Part II.

Named sub-contracts

2.28   JCT Ltd publishes a suite of three forms for use with named sub-contractors:

- ICSub/NAM: the form of tender and agreement, comprising three parts, the invitation to tender ICSub/NAM/IT, the tender ICSub/NAM/T, and the agreement ICSub/NAM/A;

- ICSub/NAM/C: the conditions of contract between the main contractor and the named sub-contractor;

- ICSub/NAM/E: the warranty between the named sub-contractor and the employer.

2.29   If it is anticipated that named sub-contractors will be used, then either the sub-contractor should be named in the bills (or specification/schedules of work), in which case details of the sub-contract are sent to the contractor at tender stage, or a provisional sum is included as described under Schedule 2 paragraph 5. The 'Sub-contract Documents' are defined under the Tender and Agreement fourth recital as comprising ICSub/NAM, ICSub/NAM/C 'together with the JCT Amendments identified in the Invitation to Tender … and the Numbered Documents'. The 'Numbered Documents', which describe the 'Sub-contract Works' to be carried out, must be listed in the ICSub/NAM/A contract particulars. No detailed description is given of what the documents might be: in practice they are likely to comprise drawings, specifications, bill of quantities, schedules, etc., which will have been prepared by the contract administrator. If the named sub-contractor is involved in design, they will also include information prepared and submitted with the tender by the sub-contractor.

2.30   ICSub/NAM/C clause 1·3 sets out definitions of terms used in the sub-contract documents. Clause 2·5 states that, in the event of any conflict, the terms of ICSub/NAM/T would take precedence over terms in any of the other sub-contract documents. If any conflict arises between the terms of the main contract and the terms of the sub-contract documents then the latter will prevail. ICSub/NAM/C contains similar provisions to IC11 regarding the correction of errors, etc. Where there are inconsistencies in or between the sub-contract documents, the contractor must issue directions to correct them (ICSub/NAM/C cl 2·10).

Use of documents

Interpretation, definitions

2.31   Clause 1·1 of the conditions sets out definitions of terms that are used throughout the contract. Some further and more detailed definitions are embodied in the text of clauses, for example 'All Risks Insurance' and 'Joint Names Policy' are defined at the beginning of clause 6·8. Clause 1·4 defines what is meant by reference to a 'person', or to 'legislation', and also includes a gender bias clause. Section 1 of the form also includes items which were first introduced by Amendment 12 to IFC84. Those regarding notices and periods of time were required by the HGCRA 1996 and restate its requirements relating to the calculation of periods of days and the serving of notices (cl 1·5 and 1·7). Clause 1·7·2 allows the parties to state that certain communications, to be identified in the contract particulars, may be made electronically. The parties may also agree the exact format for the electronic communication. It should also be noted that the contract sets out specific requirements for notices in some situations, for example termination (cl 8·2).

2.32   Clause 1·6 was introduced to the form in response to the coming into effect of the Contracts (Rights of Third Parties) Act 1999. In broad terms, this Act created rights for persons not a party to a contract to bring an action for breach of a contract, where that contract expressly gave a benefit, or purported to give a benefit, to that person. This clause prevents any such claims being brought by making it clear that the contract confers no rights on third parties.

2.33   Clause 1·12 states that the contract shall be governed by English law. This would apply even if the contract was signed, or the work was carried out, in another jurisdiction.

Priority of contract documents

2.34   Clause 1·3 states 'nothing contained in the Contract Bills/Specifications/Work Schedules nor anything in any Framework Agreement, shall override or modify the Agreement or these Conditions'. If this clause was not included, the position under common law would be the reverse; in other words, anything specifically agreed and included in a document would normally override any standard provisions in a printed form.

2.35   If the parties wish to agree to any special terms that differ in any way from the printed conditions, then the amendments will need to be made to the form. This could be done either through amending the clauses themselves, or by inserting an additional article referring to the special terms, which should be appended to the form. The article could take a similar form to that formerly used by the JCT to incorporate separately published amendments. However, attempting to amend standard forms is very unwise without expert advice as the consequential effects are difficult to predict. Deleting clause 1·3 could be particularly unwise as it may have unintended effects on other parts of the contract.

Errors in the contract bills

2.36   The contract requires that any error in the contract bills shall be corrected (cl 2·12·2). The correction requires an instruction of the contract administrator (cl 2·13·1) and is treated as described below.

Inconsistencies, errors or omissions

2.37   Clause 2·13 requires the contract administrator to issue instructions in regard to: inconsistencies, errors or omissions in or between the contract documents, the CDP documents, and in or between any further instructions or information issued to the contractor; or any departure from the agreed method for preparing any bills of quantities.

2.38   If the contractor finds any such omissions or inconsistencies it must immediately give written notice to the contract administrator (cl 2·13·3·1). If the inconsistency is within or between CDP documents, or within the employer's requirements and not dealt with in the proposals (in which case the proposals prevail), then the contractor must make written proposals for the necessary amendments (cl 2·13·3·2). The contractor is not under any express obligation to search for them, although generally it would be in the contractor's interest to do so, and a certain amount of vigilance could be expected under the normal duty to use reasonable skill and care. Nevertheless, it is the responsibility of the consultants to identify such problems, and the contract administrator's duty to issue the necessary instructions. If the instruction results in a change to the quantity or quality of the work, or to any restrictions imposed by the employer, then the contractor may be entitled to additional payment (cl 2·14), except where the correction is required as a result of an error etc. in the CDP documents (other than the employer's requirements), or through its failure to comply with the CDM Regulations. In addition, the instruction may give rise to a claim for an extension of time (cl 2·20·2) and for loss and/or expense (cl 4·18·2).

Effect of instructions to correct errors, etc.

2.39   With regard to quality and quantity of work, clause 4·1 sets out details as to priority between documents (other than the form itself). If bills are used, the quality and quantity of work shown is the work which is to be provided, even if the other documents (e.g. drawings) give different information. Where there are no bills, but the specification or work schedules give quantities, the quantity and quality shown would override any conflicting information in other documents. Where there are no bills, and no quantities given in the specification/schedules, the quality and quantity of the work 'shall be that set out in the contract documents taken together, provided that if work stated or shown on the Contract Drawings is inconsistent with the description (if any) of that work in the Specification/Work Schedules, then that stated or shown on the Contract Drawings shall prevail'. In broad terms, the drawing will take precedence over other documents if those documents do not contain any quantities.

CDP documents

2.40   Where any clause 2·13 instruction varies the quality or quantity of work as determined from clause 4·1, then this is to be treated as a variation, except that there is to be no adjustment for errors/discrepancies within or between any CDP documents, other than the requirements (cl 2·14·1, ICD11 only), nor should any extension of time be awarded. This means that there would be an adjustment for corrections to the requirements themselves. It also implies that discrepancies between the requirements and the proposals are also to be treated in this way, but it is suggested that, in cases of conflict, i.e. where the proposals do not meet the requirements, the contractor would be liable for losses due to the error, at least to the extent that the use of reasonable skill and care in preparing the proposals would have avoided it (see also paragraph 3.7).

Divergences from statutory requirements

2.41   The contractor and the contract administrator are both required to notify each other of any discrepancy or divergence between any of the clause 2·13 documents, or any instruction requiring a variation, and any statutory requirement as defined under clause 1·1 (cl 2·15·1). Where the discrepancy relates to the CDP documents, the contractor must inform the contract administrator of its proposed amendment to deal with the discrepancy. In all cases the contract administrator must issue instructions to deal with the problem. Where the divergence relates to the CDP documents, the contract states that the contractor must comply at no extra cost to the employer, unless the divergence results from a change in statutory requirements since the base date. In all other cases the instruction is treated as a variation (cl 2·15·2). The effect of this clause is that the costs will be borne by the contractor in situations where the divergence is between the employer's requirements and statute, as well as between the contractor's proposals and statute.

Custody and control of documents

2.42   The contract documents remain in the custody of the employer, and must be available for inspection by the contractor at all reasonable times (cl 2·8·1). The contract administrator should retain a copy for reference throughout the life of the contract. The contractor must be provided with one certified copy of the contract (including all 'the Contract Documents') and two further copies of the contract drawings and the contract bills/specification/work schedules (cl 2·8·2). It does not state when this should be done, but it would be good practice to arrange for the contractor to have the copies prior to work starting on site. Although it is frequently done in practice, there is no need to sign two copies of the contract. It is easy to make minor mistakes when filling out two copies of the form, and it is safer to have one definitive set of contract documents, with certified copies made as required.

2.43   The documents provided must not be used for any purpose other than the works, and the details of the rates or prices are not to be divulged (cl 2·8·3). Unlike SBC11, the form does not require the contractor to keep a set of contract documents on site; if this is required it may be sensible to include such a provision in the tender documents.

Assignment and third party rights

Assignment

2.44   Clause 7·1 states that neither the employer nor the contractor may 'assign this Contract or any rights thereunder' without the written consent of the other. Assignment without consent of the other party is grounds for termination (cl 8·4·1·4 and 8·9·1·3).

Third party rights/warranties

2.45   Until the Contracts (Rights of Third Parties) Act 1999 came into force, it was a rule of English law that only the two parties to a contract had the right to bring an action to enforce its terms (termed 'privity of contract'). The Contracts (Rights of Third Parties) Act has changed the fundamental rules of law relating to privity, in that it entitles third parties to enforce a right under a contract, where the term in question was to provide a benefit to that third party. The third party could be specifically named, or could be of an identified class of people. The effect of this Act is therefore to open the door to the possibility of claims being brought by a range of persons, in some cases persons that the parties to the contract may never have considered.

2.46   The Act, however, allows for parties to agree that their contract will not be subject to its provisions, and many standard forms adopt this course in order to limit the parties' liability.

IC11 takes this approach and, under clause 1·6, states 'nothing in this Contract confers or is intended to confer any right to enforce any of its terms on any person who is not a party to it'. The contract therefore by this clause 'contracts out' of any effects of the Act. (In the light of the above, it is important to note that the effects of deleting or amending this clause would be significant.) As an alternative to 'third party rights' the form makes provision for the employer to arrange for collateral warranties. The warranties run 'alongside' the main contract and create a contractual relationship between one of the parties to the main contract and a third party.

Warranties

2.47   IC11 refers to five forms of collateral warranty (cl 7·4–7·6) as follows:

- CWa/P&T: for use where a contractor is required to give a warranty to a purchaser or tenant of the building works (cl 7·4);

- CWa/F: for use where a contractor is required to give a warranty to a company providing finance for the building works (cl 7·5);

- SCWa/P&T or SCWa/F: for use where a sub-contractor is required to give a warranty to a purchaser/tenant or funder (cl 7·6);

- SCWa/E: where a sub-contractor is required to give a warranty to the employer (cl 7·6).

2.48   Under the system of 'collateral warranties' the contractor or sub-contractor must enter into a warranty separately with each beneficiary. The beneficiaries are identified in Part 2 of the contract particulars.

2.49   There are some things to note about this system. The contractor's liability to a purchaser or tenant extends to the reasonable costs of repair, renewal or reinstatement, but does not include other losses unless so stated in the contract particulars (CWa/P&T cl 1·1·2), in which case the liability will be limited to a stated maximum amount. The contractor's liability is also limited by net contribution clauses (CWa/P&T cl 1·3). Under the arrangement, the contractor is entitled to rely on any term in the contract should any action be brought against it by a third party (CWa/P&T cl 1·4). Where there is a contractor's designed portion, the contractor is required to provide evidence of its professional indemnity insurance to any person possessing rights under the Third Party Rights Schedule (CWa/P&T cl 5). The rights may be assigned by the purchaser or tenant without the contractor's consent to another person, and by that person to a further person, but beyond this no further assignment is permitted (CWa/P&T cl 6).

2.50   In the case of the funder, except for the inclusion of a net contribution clause (CWa/F cl 1·1), no limit is placed upon the extent of the contractor's liability. As above, the contractor is entitled to rely on any term in the contract should any action be brought by the funder (CWa/F), and the rights may be assigned by the funder without the contractor's consent to another person, and by that person to a further person, but beyond this no further assignment is permitted (CWa/F). The form also sets out various 'stepping in' rights which may be exercised by the funder in the event that it terminates its finance agreement with the employer.

Procedure with respect to warranties

2.51   Where collateral warranties are required, the contractor must execute the stipulated warranties within 14 days of receipt of a notice from the employer (cl 7·4 and 7·5).

2.52   With respect to warranties from sub-contractors, Part 2 Section E of the contract particulars must be completed (cl 7·6). The requirement for obtaining warranties states that:

> Where Part 2 of the Contract Particulars provides for the giving by any sub-contractor of a Collateral Warranty to a Purchaser, Tenant or Funder, or to the Employer, the Contractor shall, within 21 days from receipt of the Employer's notice identifying the relevant sub-contractor, type of warranty and beneficiary, comply with the Contract Documents as to obtaining such warranties in the form SCWa/P&T, SCWa/F or SCWa/E (as the case may be), completed in accordance with Part 2 of the Contract Particulars and subject to any amendments proposed by any such sub-contractor and approved by the Contractor and the Employer, such approval not to be unreasonably delayed or withheld.

2.53   It should be noted that this is not, of itself, a requirement for the contractor to obtain the warranties, nor is it even (as with GCWks1) a requirement to use reasonable endeavours to obtain the warranties – it is simply a requirement to comply with the contract conditions. The contractor is, however, required to include provisions as necessary in sub-contracts in respect of the execution of required warranties (cl 3·6·5).

3 Obligations of the contractor

3.1   The contractor's paramount obligation is to 'carry out and complete the Works'. This obligation, which is stated in Article 1, reinforced in clauses 2·1 and 2·2, and amplified in clause 4·1, is discussed in detail below. In addition, the contractor has important obligations in relation to progress and programming, discussed in Chapter 4, and in regard to insurance matters, discussed in Chapter 8. Additional obligations may also arise from the optional supplemental provisions (Schedule 5). The contractor's main obligations under IC11 and ICD11 are summarised in Figure 6.

Figure 6 Key obligations of the contractor

2·1	to carry out and complete the works in compliance with the contract documents, including the design of the CDP
2·4	to begin the works on the date of possession and to proceed regularly and diligently and complete on or before the date for completion
2·7·1	to permit the employer to carry out work not forming part of the contract
2·9	to correct any setting out errors
2·10·2 (ICD11 only)	to provide contractor's design documents and related information
2·19·1	to notify the contract administrator whenever it becomes reasonably apparent that the progress of the works is being or is likely to be delayed
2·23·2	to pay the employer liquidated damages for failure to complete by the completion date
2·30	to make good defects scheduled by the contract administrator at the end of the rectification period
2·32 (ICD11 only)	to provide as-built drawings of the CDP
3·2	to keep upon the site 'at all reasonable times' a competent 'person-in-charge'
3·6	to ensure that any sub-contract includes specified conditions
3·7 & Schedule 2	to enter into sub-contracts with named persons
3·8	to forthwith comply with all instructions issued by the contract administrator
3·18·2 & 3·19	to comply with the CDM Regulations
4·3·2	to provide the contract administrator with all documentation necessary for the final valuation
6·1 & 6·2	to indemnify the employer and to take out effective insurance against injury to persons and property
6·4	to take out insurance against personal injury or property damage
6·5	to take out insurance for liability of employer as required
6·7 & Schedule 1	to take out insurance against loss or damage to the works as required
6·13	to comply with the Joint Fire Code where it applies
7·4–7·6	to comply with requirements regarding warranties

The works

3.2   The works that the contractor undertakes to carry out will be as briefly described in the first recital of IC11, and as shown or described in the contract documents. It is therefore important that the entry in the first recital clearly identifies the nature and scope of the proposed work, and that the descriptions of the works set out the required standards and quality of workmanship and materials fully and accurately. It should be noted that the contractor's obligation to carry out the works extends to any changes made to those works, as stipulated in Article 1, provided that these changes are made in accordance with the terms of the contract.

Contractor's design obligation

3.3   IC11 is essentially a work and materials contract, and makes no reference to the main contractor carrying out design. The only mechanism within IC11 whereby some of the design responsibility can be allocated to a specialist company is through the use of the provisions for named sub-contractors, and the contractor will not be liable for their design errors (therefore a collateral warranty will be essential). This allocation of design liability must, of course, be approved by the employer before the named sub-contractor is approached, and preferably before the contract administrator's appointment is agreed with the employer, as otherwise the contract administrator will remain fully responsible for all aspects of that design (Figure 7).

3.4   The new ICD11 incorporates provisions for the contractor's design of part or parts of the works, alongside those for the appointment of named sub-contractors. The contractor's

Figure 7 Watchpoints: contractor's design

- The contractor's liability for providing the CDP work is limited to the use of reasonable skill and care (cl 2·34·1).
- Level of professional indemnity insurance must be stated in the contract particulars, otherwise none will be required (cl 6·16·1).
- It is unclear what level of design responsibility the contractor will have for any design not stated to be included in the contractor's designed portion, or whether the contractor is required to insure for this.
- In cases where the contractor's proposals are found not to comply with the employer's requirements, it is unclear which takes precedence (seventh recital, cl 2·34·4).
- Integration of the design work remains the responsibility of the contract administrator (cl 2·1·2).
- The tender documents should state the exact scope and format of the information to be included in the contractor's proposals.
- The contractor is obliged to submit further 'reasonably necessary' information 'as and when necessary' (cl 2·10·2 and 2·10·3). It is suggested that the exact information required and dates for submission are set out in the contract documents.
- Information required to be submitted at practical completion should be set out in the contract documents (cl 2·32).
- The employer may make changes to the employer's requirements (which may result in changes to the contract sum and the completion date), but otherwise there is no power to order changes to the contractor's proposals provided they comply with the requirements (cl 3·11·3).

design obligation is set out under clause 2·1, which states that 'in compliance with the Contract Documents, the Construction Phase Plan (where applicable) and other Statutory Requirements … the Contractor shall … complete the design for the Contractor's Designed Portion'. As above, the allocation of design responsibility must be agreed with the client. It should be noted that with ICD11 the named sub-contractor should not be required to carry out work within the contractor's designed portion.

3.5   The design requirements will have been set out in the employer's requirements and sent out with the tender documents (fourth recital). The contractor will have submitted a proposal containing a design solution with its tender (the contractor's proposals, sixth recital) although, depending on the information requested, this may not be fully detailed. Some of the design may therefore remain to be finalised after the contract is entered into. Somewhat surprisingly, clause 2·1 does not state that the design should be completed in accordance with the employer's requirements. However this appears to be required under clause 2·34·1 and, on balance, it is likely that this obligation would be implied. Nevertheless, it may be wise to clarify this in the tender documents.

3.6   Clause 2·34·4 makes it clear that the contractor is not responsible for the contents of the employer's requirements, or for verifying the adequacy of any design contained within them. This clause is included to prevent such an obligation being implied, as it was in the case of *Co-operative Insurance Society* v *Henry Boot*. Although it is not entirely clear, it is unlikely to prevent the implication of a 'duty to warn' regarding any other aspects of the consultant team's design, for example where the design is varied through an instruction (for an instance of this see the earlier case of *Plant Construction* v *Clive Adams*).

Co-operative Insurance Society v *Henry Boot Scotland and others* (2002) 84 Con LR 164

The Co-operative Insurance Society (the Society) engaged the contractor Henry Boot on an amended version of JCT80 incorporating the Designed Portion Supplement, where the relevant terms are virtually identical to those of WCD98. During construction, problems arose where soil and water flooded into a basement excavation. An engineer had originally been employed by the Society to prepare a concept design for the structure, and Henry Boot had developed the design and prepared working drawings. The Society brought claims against Henry Boot and the engineers. Henry Boot argued that its liability was limited to the preparation of the working drawings. The judge, however, took the view that completing the design of the contiguous bored pile walls included examining the design at the point that it was taken over, assessing the assumptions on which it was based and forming a view as to whether they were appropriate.

Plant Construction v *Clive Adams Associates and JMH Construction Services* [2000] BLR 137 (CA)

Ford Motor Company engaged Plant on a JCT WCD contract to design and construct two pits for engine mount rigs at Ford's research and engineering centre in Essex. Part of the work included underpinning an existing column, and in the course of the work temporary support was required to the column and the floor above. JMH was sub-contracted to carry out this concrete work. Ford's own engineer gave instructions regarding the temporary supports, which comprised four Acrow props. JMH and Plant's engineers, Clive Adams Associates, felt the props to be inadequate and discussed this on site. The support was installed as instructed and failed, so that a large part of a concrete floor slab collapsed. Plant settled with Ford, and brought a claim against JMH and Clive Adams (who settled). The court found that the duties of the sub-contractor included warning of any aspect of the design it knew to be unsafe. It reserved its opinion on whether the duty would extend to unsafe aspects it ought to have known about, or design errors that were not unsafe.

3.7   As discussed above (at paragraph 2.40), the seventh recital states 'the Employer has examined the Contractor's Proposals and, subject to the Conditions, is satisfied that they appear to meet the Employer's Requirements', which implies that, in so far as the design has been finalised at the time of acceptance of tender, then the employer has accepted the solution. It might be possible to argue that the employer could not be held to have accepted defects in the design which a reasonable inspection would not have revealed. An example might be the design of a roof truss where, without a detailed double checking of calculations, it would not be possible to ascertain whether the truss would be structurally sound. In addition, under clause 2·34·1 the contractor is liable for any inadequacy in the design of the proposals, and the employer's requirements would be taken into account (along with other factors) in assessing what was inadequate. The contractor would therefore remain responsible for achieving this, whatever the proposals showed. Nevertheless, the recital is problematic from the point of view of the employer and is sometimes deleted.

Ad hoc approaches

3.8   If any attempts are made to place a design obligation on the contractor using 'ad hoc' methods, e.g. through the use of clauses in the bills or by the inclusion of a performance specification, it would depend on the particular circumstances whether or not this would be successful. Such methods should not be attempted without legal advice. Bearing in mind the result of the case of *Rotherham MBC* v *Frank Haslam Milan*, it is clear that a court would be unwilling to place design responsibility on a contractor in situations where a contract administrator has been employed to prepare full design and specifications.

Rotherham MBC v *Frank Haslam Milan and M J Gleeson* [1996] 78 BLR 1 (CA)

Rotherham MBC entered into a contract to build a new office block. The tender documents included a detailed specification, which stated that the hardcore for the ground floor slab could be any number of a list of materials, including 'slag'. There is more than one type of slag, including an unslaked type that expands when wet. The contractor used the unslaked type, with predictable results. Rotherham claimed that the contractor was in a breach of its duty to select a hardcore fit for purpose. However, the court found that, in situations where an employer engages a professional team to prepare a detailed specification, it is not relying on the contractor's expertise in making such decisions, and the contractor was therefore not liable.

The level of design liability

3.9   Standard forms of contract and appointment will often set out specific provisions regarding design liability, but these have to be understood in the legal context in which they operate.

A key point is whether any design liability incurred is a 'fitness for purpose' or 'reasonable skill and care' level of liability.

3.10   The Sale of Goods Act 1979 implies terms into all contracts for the sale of goods that the goods sold will be of satisfactory quality. The Unfair Contract Terms Act 1977 stipulates that this requirement cannot be excluded in any contract with a consumer, and can only be excluded in other contracts in so far as it would be reasonable to do so. If parties have included terms which purport to exclude this liability, the terms will be void. Similarly, if the use to which the goods are to be put is made clear to the seller, the seller must supply goods suitable for that use unless it is clear that the buyer is not relying on the seller's skill and judgement. So if, for example, a DIY enthusiast asks a builders' merchant for paint suitable for use on a bathroom ceiling, the merchant must supply suitable paint, regardless of what is written in the contract of sale. If, however, the buyer specifies the exact type of paint, the seller would no longer be liable as the buyer is not relying on the seller's advice.

3.11   Contracts for construction work are usually for 'work and materials' (as opposed to supply-only or install-only) and, as such, fall under the Supply of Goods and Services Act 1982. This implies similar terms to those described above in relation to any goods supplied under such a contract. Therefore, a contractor would normally be liable for providing materials fit for their intended purposes. If, however, an employer or consultant specifies particular materials, the contractor would be relieved of this liability.

3.12   The obligation to supply goods or materials fit for their intended purpose would extend to a product or structure which a contractor had agreed to design and construct (*Viking Grain Storage Ltd* v *T H White*). In all cases the liability of the contractor will be strict; in other words, the contractor will be liable if the good, element or structure is not fit for its intended use, irrespective of whether the contractor has exercised a reasonable level of skill and care in carrying out the design. This is a more onerous level of liability than that assumed by someone undertaking design services only, where they would normally be required to demonstrate that they had exercised the skill and care of a competent member of their profession. To put it the other way round, if an employer can prove that a building designed and constructed by a contractor is defective, then this will normally be sufficient to prove that there has been a breach of contract, whereas, in the case of a design professional, the employer would also have to prove that the professional had been negligent.

Viking Grain Storage Ltd v *T H White Installations Ltd* (1985) 33 BLR 103

Viking Grain entered into a contract with White to design and erect a grain drying and storage installation to handle 10,000 tonnes of grain. After it was complete, Viking commenced proceedings against the contractor claiming that, because of defects, the grain store was unfit for its intended use. The contractor, in its defence, claimed that there was no implied warranty in the contract that the finished product would be fit for purpose, and that the contractor's obligation was limited to the use of reasonable skill and care in carrying out the design. The judge decided that Viking had been relying on the contractor and, because of this reliance, there was an implied warranty that, not only the materials supplied, but the whole installation, should be fit for the required purpose. There could be no differentiation between reliance placed on the quality of the materials and on the design.

3.13   Under clause 2·34·1 of ICD11, the contractor's liability for the contractor's designed portion is limited to using the skill and care of an 'appropriate professional designer holding himself out as competent to take on work for such design'. In effect, this means that, in order to prove a breach, the employer would need to prove that the contractor had been negligent. If, for example, the contractor is required to design a heating system to heat rooms to a certain temperature and, when installed, it fails to do so, this fact alone would not be enough to prove that there had been a breach of contract. The employer would need to prove that the contractor had failed to use the skill and care expected of a professional person.

3.14   It should be noted that, where the contractor is carrying out work in connection with a dwelling, including design work, this would be subject to the Defective Premises Act 1972. This obligation is acknowledged in clause 2·34·2. The Act states that 'a person taking on work for or in connection with the provision of a dwelling … owes a duty … to see that the work which he takes on is done in a workmanlike or, as the case may be, professional manner, with proper materials and so that as regards that work the dwelling will be fit for habitation when completed' (section 1(1)). In case law, the duty has not generally been taken to be a strict or absolute warranty of fitness (*Alexander and another* v *Mercouris*), although other authorities suggest that it is a strict duty. It should be noted that, although the contractor's liability is limited to the amount stated in the contract particulars, the limitation does not apply to work in connection with a dwelling (cl 2·34·3).

Alexander and another v *Mercouris* [1979] 1 WLR 1270

This case considered when the duty arose, not its scope, but some observations are helpful, for example Lord Justice Buckley stated: 'It seems to me clear upon the language of Section 1(1) that the duty is intended to arise when a person takes on the work. The word "owes" is used in the present tense and the duty is not to ensure that the work has been done in a proper and workmanlike manner with proper materials so that the dwelling is fit for habitation when completed, but to see that the work is done in a proper and workmanlike manner with proper materials so that the work will be fit for habitation when completed. The duty is one to be performed during the carrying on of the work. The reference to the dwelling being fit for habitation indicates the intended consequence of the proper performance of the duty and provides a measure of the standard of the requisite work and materials. It is not, I think, part of the duty itself.'

Materials, goods and workmanship

3.15   Under clause 2·1 the contractor is obliged to carry out the works in a proper and workmanlike manner and in compliance with the contract documents and the construction phase plan. Clause 4·1 discusses the position where there is a conflict between the quality stipulated in different contract documents. Although the contract administrator must issue instructions to resolve the discrepancy, there could be doubt as to the contractor's original obligation as to quality, and hence whether or not the instruction would constitute a variation. Clause 4·1 therefore sets out a priority between documents. Where there is a description given in a bill of quantities, this would take precedence over any description contained in another document. Where no bill of quantities has been used, but quantities are set out in a specification or schedule of works, the quality of work should be as described in that document. In situations where bills are not used and the specification or schedules do not include quantities, the quality is that 'in the Contract Documents taken together', except that any description given in drawings would override any set out in a specification or schedule of work.

3.16   In cases not covered by the above, and in cases where the documents must be 'taken together', a court would assess what, from the point of view of an objective bystander, appeared to be the intention of the parties at the time the contract was entered into. In practical terms, care should be taken to avoid duplicating descriptions of quality. The Construction Project Information Committee (CPIC) recommendation is that the specification becomes the core document in terms of defining quality, and that the drawings, schedules and bills refer to clauses in the specification, so that careful use of the CPIC system ought to avoid conflicting descriptions appearing in different documents.

3.17   Clause 2·2·1 states:

> Where and to the extent that approval of the quality of materials or goods or of the standards of workmanship is a matter for the Architect/Contract Administrator's opinion, such quality and standards shall be to his reasonable satisfaction. To the extent that the quality of materials and goods or standards of workmanship are neither described … nor stated to be a matter for such opinion or satisfaction, they shall be of a standard appropriate to the Works.

This reflects the duty that would normally be implied by law; in other words, where the description of the standard required for any goods, materials and workmanship is (deliberately or inadvertently) incomplete, the contractor is required to provide something 'fit for purpose'. This appears to be a strict obligation (see above), rather than an obligation to use reasonable skill and care.

3.18   The phrase 'Where and to the extent that approval of the quality … is a matter for the Contract Architect/Contract Administrator's opinion, such quality and standards shall be to his reasonable satisfaction' (cl 2·2·1) means that where a correct construction of the contract documents leaves a matter regarding quality to the discretion of the contract administrator, the contractor only fulfils its obligations if the contract administrator is satisfied. It is suggested that any expression of dissatisfaction by the contract administrator must be made within a reasonable period of the carrying out of the work and not left, for example, until the work has been built in. It should be noted that the final certificate is conclusive evidence that, where the contract documents have expressly stated that the quality is to be to the approval of the contract administrator, then the contract administrator is so satisfied (cl 1·9·1·1). This would have the effect of preventing the employer from bringing a claim regarding those items of work. The contract administrator should therefore avoid using phrases such as 'to approval' or 'to the contract administrator's satisfaction' in the contract documents, as it puts the employer at some risk.

3.19   If the phrase 'or otherwise approved' is used in a specification or bill of quantities, this does not mean that the contract administrator must be prepared to consider alternatives put forward by the contractor, nor that the contract administrator must give any reasons for rejecting alternatives (*Leedsford* v *City of Bradford*). It merely gives the contract administrator the right to do so. A substitution would always constitute a variation, whether or not this phrase is present in the specification.

Leedsford Ltd v *The Lord Mayor, Alderman and Citizens of the City of Bradford* (1956) 24 BLR 45 (CA)

In a contract for the provision of a new infant school, the contract bills stated 'Artificial Stone ... The following to be obtained from the Empire Stone Company Limited, 326 Deansgate, or other approved firm'. During the course of the contract the contractor obtained quotes from other companies and sent them to the architect for approval. The architect, however, insisted that Empire Stone was used and, as Empire Stone was considerably more expensive, the contractor brought a claim for damages for breach of contract. The court dismissed the claim stating 'The builder agrees to supply artificial stone. The stone has to be Empire Stone unless the parties agree some other stone, and no other stone can be substituted except by mutual agreement. The builder fulfils his contract if he provides Empire Stone, whether the Bradford Corporation want it or not; and the Corporation Architect can say that he will approve of no other stone except the Empire Stone' (Hodson LJ at page 58).

Obligations in respect of quality of sub-contracted work

3.20   Two methods of sub-contracting are allowed for under IC11:

- sub-letting to a domestic sub-contractor selected by the contractor, but with the written consent of the contract administrator (cl 3·5);

- sub-letting to a named sub-contractor under the procedure set out in Schedule 2 paragraphs 1 to 4 (cl 3·7).

3.21   In both cases the contractor will still have ultimate responsibility for the standard of workmanship, materials and goods provided by the sub-contractor (cl 3·5) under Schedule 2 paragraph 13. With respect to named sub-contractors, the responsibility is qualified by Schedule 2 paragraph 11. This makes it clear that the contractor is not responsible to the employer for design of the named sub-contract works, or the selection of materials and goods for those works, or the satisfaction of any performance specification or requirement for the sub-contract works, in so far as the named sub-contractor has or will be carrying out these tasks. This disclaimer applies whether or not the named sub-contractor is responsible to the employer. It is therefore extremely important that the named sub-contractor enters into a warranty with the employer SCWa/E, as otherwise the employer would have no redress against the sub-contractor should the design fail.

Compliance with statute

3.22   The contractor is under a statutory duty to comply with all legislation that is relevant to the carrying out of the work, for example in respect of goods and services, building and construction regulations, and health and safety. The duty is absolute and there is no possibility of contracting out of any of the resulting obligations.

3.23   IC11 and ICD11 introduce a contractual duty in addition to the statutory duty. Clause 2·1 requires the contractor to complete the works 'in compliance with … the Statutory Requirements'. This obligation is limited by clause 2·15·3, which states that the contractor would not be contractually liable if the non-compliance resulted from carrying out work in accordance with the contract documents or further instructions issued by the contract administrator. The contractor is reimbursed for any fees or charges, unless the tender documents made it clear that the contractor was to include for these in the contract sum (cl 2·3).

3.24   If the contractor finds any divergence between what the contract requires and statutory requirements, then the contract administrator must be given immediate written notice (cl 2·15·1). The contractor is under no obligation to search for divergence, but is, of course, under a general obligation to use reasonable skill and care in carrying out the works. The contract does not state what should happen once a divergence is discovered, but the contract administrator should issue an instruction promptly to rectify the situation. The contractor may need to take immediate action in an emergency, but only in so far as is reasonably necessary to comply with statutory requirements (cl 2·16). Provided it was necessary, the work is treated as if it were a variation required by an instruction. There appears to be no obligation on the contract administrator to cover the work with an instruction, but an accurate record should be kept.

Health and safety legislation

3.25   The appropriate deletion in the contract particulars (seventh or tenth recital) should indicate whether or not the project is notifiable under the CDM Regulations. Where it is, the contractor would be obliged to give statutory notice to the Health and Safety Executive before carrying out any construction work.

3.26   Where all the CDM Regulations apply, the employer must appoint a CDM co-ordinator, who will be the contract administrator or some other person named in Article 5. If that person ceases to be the CDM co-ordinator, the employer must employ another person and notify the contractor accordingly (cl 3·19). Clause 3·18·1 places a contractual obligation on the employer to ensure that the CDM co-ordinator carries out his or her duties under the CDM Regulations. This is a wider obligation than the 'reasonable satisfaction with competence' obligation imposed by the CDM Regulations. Breach of it gives the contractor the right to terminate the contract under clause 8·9·1·4. What is more likely to happen is that the contractor will claim for an extension of time or direct loss and/or expense. An example might be where a CDM co-ordinator delays in commenting on a contractor's proposed amendment to the construction phase plan and progress is thereby delayed.

3.27   The contract assumes that the contractor will act as principal contractor, unless another firm is named (Articles 6), and it should be noted that under Article 6 this role is now extended to cover obligations under the Site Waste Management Plans Regulations 2008. Clause 3·18 places a duty on the contractor, if acting as the principal contractor, to comply with all the relevant duties set out in the CDM Regulations. It is an express requirement that the contractor must develop the construction phase plan and ensure that the employer receives it before work is commenced (cl 3·18·2).

3.28   The contractor is obliged to send any modification of the construction phase plan to the employer, the CDM co-ordinator and the contract administrator (cl 3·18·2). This may occur, for example, due to unexpected site conditions. The contractor should take the cost of developing the construction phase plan into account at tender stage, and no claims can be made for adjusting it to suit the contractor's or sub-contractor's working methods. If alterations are needed as a result of an instruction requiring a variation then the costs are included in valuing the variation, and the alterations may be taken into account in assessing an application for extension of time.

3.29   Breach of any CDM duty is grounds for termination under clause 8·4·1·5, but the warning notice still has to be given. Any breach is covered, however, provided termination is not unreasonable or vexatious, and the contract administrator should consider any breach that might lead to action being taken against the employer as a serious matter. If work needs to be postponed or other instructions given due to a breach by the contractor then there would be no entitlement to an extension of time or direct loss and/or expense.

4   **Possession and completion**

4.1   The date of possession or commencement and the date for completion of the work are key dates in any building contract, and IC11 requires a 'Date of Possession' and a 'Date for Completion' to be inserted in the contract particulars. IC11 also offers the facility for the work to be carried out in phases. If this is required, then the work must be split into clearly identified 'Sections', and a separate 'Date of Possession' and 'Date for Completion' entered for each section. The contractor is required to take possession on the date for possession, and complete by the date for completion, and if it fails to do so it may be liable to pay liquidated damages. There is provision for deferring the date of possession, and extending the completion date. If Supplemental Provision 3 is incorporated, this could also result in an agreed adjustment to the completion date. If the work is divided into sections, provisions for commencement, completion, deferment and extension operate independently for each section.

4.2   It is good practice to give the contractor calendar dates at the time of tendering and not vague indications such as 'to be agreed' or 'eight weeks after approval by'. The start date and the time of year that the work is carried out will affect the contractor's costs, so that, unless clear dates are given, it will be impossible to compare tenders with accuracy. In addition, by the time it comes to executing the contract documents, the contractor may well protest that the dates now being proposed are not those that had been assumed in the tender, and may insist that the contract sum is adjusted.

4.3   In the event that work is started without proper agreement over dates, the contract will be subject to the Supply of Goods and Services Act 1982, which states that the work should be completed within a reasonable time. It is unlikely, however, that once the job is underway the parties will be able to agree what a reasonable time might be.

4.4   The named sub-contractor must carry out its work in accordance with the programme agreed in the sub-contract documents (ICSub/NAM/C cl 2·2). The contractor is informed in the invitation to tender of the expected dates between which its work can be commenced (ICSub/NAM/IT cl 9). The sub-contractor is required to give detailed information on its requirements in respect of programming in its tender (ICSub/NAM/T cl 1). These details include the periods required for the preparation of drawings, for the incorporation of any comments, for fabrication and delivery, for notification of commencement and for carrying out the work on site. In the case of the latter, there is provision to set out separate periods where the work is to be carried out in sections.

Possession by the contractor

4.5   Possession of the site is a fundamental term of the contract. Failure to give the contractor possession is a serious breach by the employer, which may amount to repudiation, and therefore give the contractor the right to treat the contract as at an end. Giving possession of only part of the site, or in stages, could amount to a breach unless this intention has been made clear in the contract documents (*Whittal Builders* v *Chester-le-Street DC*). Such breaches would constitute an 'impediment' under clause 2·20·6 and 4·18·4, entitling the contractor to claim an extension of time and direct loss and/or expense.

Whittal Builders Co. Ltd v *Chester-le-Street District Council* (1987) 40 BLR 82

Whittal Builders contracted with the Council on JCT63 to carry out modernisation work to 90 dwellings. The contract documents did not mention the possibility of phasing, but the Council gave the contractor possession of the houses in a piecemeal manner. Even though work of this nature was frequently phased, the judge nevertheless found that the employer was in breach of contract for not giving the contractor possession of all 90 dwellings at the start of the contract, and the contractor was entitled to damages.

4.6   Degree of possession is such that there must be no interference that prevents the contractor from working in whatever way or sequence it chooses. With most jobs this means that the contractor must be given clear possession of the whole site up until practical completion. Where clear possession is not intended, then the tender documents should set out in detail the restrictions and the contract must be amended accordingly. Should the employer wish to use any part of the works for any purpose during the time that the contractor has possession, this should also be made clear in the tender documents, otherwise it can only be with the agreement of the contractor (cl 2·6).

4.7   If clause 2·5 has been stated in the contract particulars to apply, then it is possible for the employer to defer possession of the works or any section without the agreement of the contractor (it is important to note that, if the correct deletion is not made, the clause will not apply). The clause allows for deferment for a period not exceeding six weeks; if a shorter maximum period is preferred, this must be stated in the tender documents and inserted in the contract particulars (cl 2·5). Where the work is split into sections, different maximum periods may be entered for each section. Any delay beyond the period stated is a breach of contract. It is the employer's right to defer possession, therefore the notice to the contractor should be written by the employer, on the advice of the contract administrator. If possession is deferred, the contractor may claim an extension of time (cl 2·20·3) and direct loss and/or expense (cl 4·17·1).

4.8   The parties are, of course, always free to renegotiate the terms of any contract. Therefore, if there is a delay in giving possession which is longer than the amount stated in the contract particulars, the parties may have to agree a new date of possession, usually with financial compensation to the contractor. Any further delay beyond the agreed date would, of course, be a breach.

Progress

4.9   It would normally be implied into a construction contract that a contractor will proceed 'regularly and diligently', and this is an express term in IC11 (cl 2·4). The contractor is free to organise its own working methods and sequences of operations, with the qualification that it must comply with statutory requirements and the construction phase plan. This has been held to be the case even where the contractor's chosen sequencing may cause extra cost to the employer with the operation of fluctuation provisions (*GLC* v *Cleveland Bridge and Engineering*).

Greater London Council v *Cleveland Bridge and Engineering Co.* (1986) 34 BLR 50 (CA)

The Greater London Council (GLC) employed Cleveland Bridge to fabricate and install gates and gate arms for the Thames Barrier. The specially drafted contract provided dates by which Cleveland Bridge had to complete certain parts of the works. Clause 51 was a fluctuations provision which allowed for adjustments to be made to the contract sum if, for example, the rates of wages or prices of materials rose or fell during the course of the contract. The clause also contained the phrase 'provided that no account shall be taken of any amount by which any cost incurred by the Contractor has been increased by the default or negligence of the Contractor'. The contract was lengthy, and Cleveland Bridge left part of the work to be carried out at the very end of the period, but delivered the gates on time. The result was that the GLC had to pay a large amount of fluctuations in respect of the work done at the last minute. The GLC argued that the contractor had failed to proceed regularly and diligently, and therefore was in default. The court held that even if the slowness of the contractor's progress might at certain points have given the employer the right to terminate the contractor under the termination provisions, this would not, in itself, be a breach of contract as referred to in clause 51. The contractor could organise the work any way it wished provided it completed on time: it was therefore owed the full amount of the fluctuations.

4.10   There is no requirement under IC11 for the contractor to produce a master programme. Of course, there is nothing to prevent such a requirement being introduced through the bill of quantities or specification, but it should be made clear that this will not be a contract document. If it is to be required, then it would be wise to stipulate that the contractor submits it before the contract is entered into. It is notoriously difficult to extract programmes from contractors once work has commenced – sometimes the programme when finally produced can include an element of post-rationalisation to show that early events caused problems and delays. If requested, it is also advisable to ask for a critical path analysis, since it can otherwise be difficult to assess the effect of delays.

4.11   One of the functions of a programme is to indicate when information will be needed from the contract administrator, and if the information release schedule is not used it would be open to the contractor to submit such a programme, even if one were not requested. Again, the programme would not be contractually binding. It should be remembered that even if the contractor's programme shows an intention to complete early, there is no implied duty on the employer to enable the contractor to achieve this early completion (*Glenlion Construction* v *The Guinness Trust*) and, in particular, the contract administrator's obligation to provide information would not be assessed against this programme. It would be sensible, however, to notify the employer if an early finish is shown, as the employer should be alert to the possibility that it may receive the building earlier than had been anticipated.

Glenlion Construction Ltd v *The Guinness Trust* (1987) 39 BLR 89

The Guinness Trust employed Glenlion Construction to carry out works in relation to a residential development at Bromley, Kent. The contract was on JCT63, which required the contractor to complete 'on or before' the date for completion, and to provide a programme. Disputes arose which went to arbitration and several questions of law regarding the contractor's programme were subsequently raised in court. The contractor later claimed loss and expense on the ground that it was prevented from economic working and achieving the early completion date shown on its programme only by failure of the architect to provide necessary information and instructions to the dates shown. The court decided that Glenlion was entitled to complete before the date for completion, whether or not it was contractually bound to produce a programme and whether or not it did in fact produce one. Glenlion was therefore entitled to carry out the works in a way which would achieve an earlier completion date. However, there was no implied obligation that the employer (or the architect) should perform its obligations so as to enable the contractor to complete by any earlier completion date shown on the programme.

Completion

4.12   The most important reason for giving an exact completion date in a building contract is that it provides a fixed point from which damages may be payable in the event of non-completion. Generally, in construction contracts the damages are 'liquidated', and typically are fixed at a rate per week of overrun.

4.13   The contractor is obliged to complete the works by the completion date, and in general accepts the risk of all events that might prevent completion by this date, except to the extent that the contract provides otherwise. The contractor would normally be relieved of this obligation if the employer caused delays or in some way prevented completion. In order to avoid situations arising where the contractor is no longer bound by the completion date, most contracts contain provisions allowing for the adjustment of the completion date in the event of certain delays caused by the employer.

4.14   In contracts it is sometimes essential that completion is achieved by a particular date and failure would mean that the result is worthless. This is sometimes referred to as 'time is of the essence'. Breach of such a term would be considered a fundamental breach, and would give the employer the right to terminate performance of the contract, and treat all its own obligations as at an end. The expression 'time is of the essence' is seldom, if ever, applicable to building contracts such as IC11, as the inclusion of extensions of time and liquidated damages provisions implies that the parties intended otherwise.

4.15   In IC11 a 'Date for Completion' is inserted in the contract particulars, which is the date agreed at the time of entering into the contract. If the sectional completion provisions are used, a separate date will be stated for each section. IC11 provides for the granting of extensions of time, and refers throughout the form to the 'Completion Date', which is the date for completion, or any extended date following an extension of time. There is no provision for reducing the contract period to a date earlier than the date for completion,

Figure 8 Completion and liquidated damages

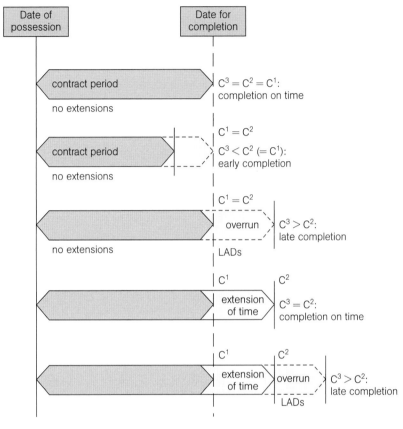

KEY
C^1 = date for completion (entered in contract particulars)
C^2 = completion date (as adjusted by extension of time)
C^3 = practical completion (as certified by contract administrator)
LADs = liquidated and ascertained damages

even when substantial work is omitted. If the contractor fails to complete by the completion date, liquidated damages become payable (see Figure 8).

Extensions of time

Principle

4.16   The main reason for including extension of time provisions in a building contract is to preserve the employer's right to liquidated damages in the event that the contractor fails to complete on time due, in part, to some action for which the employer is responsible. If no such provisions were included, and a delay occurred that was caused by the employer, this would in effect be a breach of contract by the employer and the contractor would no longer be bound to complete by the completion date (*Peak Construction* v *McKinney Foundations*). The employer would therefore lose the right to liquidated damages, even though much of the blame for the delay rests with the contractor. The phrase 'time at large' is often used to describe this situation. However, this is, strictly speaking, a misuse of the phrase as, in most cases, the contractor would remain under an obligation to complete within a reasonable time.

Peak Construction (Liverpool) Ltd v *McKinney Foundations Ltd* (1970) 1 BLR 111 (CA)

Peak Construction was the main contractor on a project to construct a multi-storey block of flats for Liverpool Corporation. The main contract was not on any of the standard forms, but was drawn up by the Corporation. McKinney Foundations Ltd was the sub-contractor nominated to design and construct the piling. After the piling was complete and the sub-contractor had left the site, serious defects were discovered in one of the piles and, following further investigation, minor defects were found in several other piles. Work was halted while the best strategy for remedial work was debated between the parties. The city surveyor did not accept the initial remedial proposals, and it was agreed that an independent engineer would prepare a proposal. The Corporation refused to agree to accept his decision in advance, and delayed making the appointment. Altogether it was 58 weeks before work resumed (although the remedial work took only six weeks) and the main contractor brought a claim against the sub-contractor for damages. The Official Referee at first instance found that the entire 58 weeks constituted delay caused by the nominated sub-contractor and awarded £40,000 damages for breach of contract, based in part on liquidated damages which the Corporation had claimed from the contractors. McKinney appealed, and the Court of Appeal found that the 58-week delay could not possibly entirely be due to the sub-contractor's breach, but was in part caused by the tardiness of the Corporation. This being the case, and as there were no provisions in the contract for extending time for delay on the part of the Corporation, it lost its right to claim liquidated damages, and this component of the damages awarded against the sub-contractor was disallowed. Even if the contract had contained such a provision, the failure of the architect to exercise it would have prevented the Corporation from claiming liquidated damages. The only remedy would have been for the Corporation to prove what damages it had suffered as a result of the breach.

Procedure

4.17   In IC11 the provisions for granting an extension of time are under clauses 2·19 and 2·20. The contractor must give written notice 'forthwith' to the contract administrator when it appears that progress is being or is likely to be delayed. The notice must be given whether or not completion is likely to be delayed, whatever the cause might be (i.e. the requirement to give a notice is not limited to circumstances where the contractor is claiming an extension of time). The notice should set out the cause of the delay, but the contractor is not required to identify whether the cause is a 'Relevant Event' listed in clause 2·20, and the contract administrator's obligation to issue an appropriate extension of time is not dependent on the contractor having done so. However, the contractor is required to provide the contract administrator with any information reasonably required (cl 2·19·4·2), and to issue a further notice if there is any further delay (cl 2·19·5).

4.18   Following notification, the contract administrator must then assess the delay caused and issue an extension of time, if appropriate. The extension can only be given in relation to delay caused by events listed in clause 2·20. Although the point has not been decided by the courts in relation to IC11, it appears that, prior to the completion date, notification is a condition precedent to the award of an extension of time; in other words, the contract administrator may not issue an extension unless a valid notice has been given. In any event, it would be difficult to make an assessment in the absence of any information from the contractor, and clause 2·19·4·2 makes it clear that the award of an extension of time is dependent on the provision of reasonably necessary information.

4.19   In regard to relevant events the following points should be noted:

- failure to supply information is not specifically listed, but would constitute a default by the contract administrator under clause 2·20·6;

- statutory undertaker's work (cl 2·20·7) only covers situations where work is done in pursuance of statutory duties. If directly engaged by the employer this comes under clause 2·20·6;

- weather has to be exceptional and adverse (i.e. not that which would be expected at the time of year in question, cl 2·20·8);

- specified perils (cl 2·20·9) can, under certain circumstances, include events caused by the contractor's own negligence;

- a very wide protection is afforded with respect to strikes (cl 2·20·11), and not simply those directly affecting the works, but also those causing difficulties in preparation and transportation of goods and materials. Such strikes will not necessarily be confined to the UK and, given the current extent of overseas imports, the effects could be considerable. It was generally considered, however, that the fuel tax blockades in 2000 were not an event which fell under this clause (or indeed any other relevant event);

- 'force majeure' (cl 2·20·13) is a French term used 'with reference to all circumstances independent of the will of man, and which it is not in his power to control'. It includes Acts of God and other matters outside the control of the parties. However, many items under this category, e.g. strikes, fire and weather, are dealt with elsewhere in the contract.

4.20   There is no time limit on when the decision regarding an extension of time should be made (cl 2·19·1). However, the clause states 'as soon as he is able' and, as failure to grant an extension properly due could result in time being 'at large', the contract administrator should take care to deal with the matter reasonably quickly. It certainly would be unwise to set the matter to one side until the end of the project. The clause does not require the contract administrator to notify the contractor if the decision is that no extension of time is due, but it would be reasonable to make the contractor aware of the position. There is also no obligation to explain why any extension has been awarded.

4.21   The contract administrator may award further extensions of time in respect of certain events which occur after the date for completion or any extended date, i.e. when the contractor is in 'culpable delay' (*Balfour Beatty* v *Chestermont Properties*), and must award one if due, irrespective of whether any notice has been issued by the contractor (cl 2·19·3). In this event the extension is added onto the date that has passed, referred to as the 'net' method of extension. The range of events is less than those for which an extension can be awarded before the completion date has passed: it does not include many neutral events, such as delays by the specified perils or the contractor's inability, for reasons beyond its control, to secure necessary labour.

Balfour Beatty Building Ltd v *Chestermont Properties Ltd* (1993) 62 BLR 1

In a contract on JCT80, the works were not completed by the revised completion date and the architect issued a non-completion certificate. The architect then issued a series of variation instructions and a further extension of time, which had the effect of fixing a completion date two-and-a-half months before the first of the variation instructions. He then issued a further non-completion certificate and the employer proceeded to deduct liquidated damages. The contractor took the matter to arbitration and then appealed certain decisions on preliminary questions given by the arbitrator. The court held that the architect's power to grant an extension of time pursuant to clause 25·3·1·1 could only operate in respect of relevant events that occurred before the original or the previously fixed completion date, but the power to grant an extension under clause 25·3·3 applied to any relevant event. The architect was right to add the extension of time retrospectively (termed the 'net' method).

4.22   The contract administrator may make a further extension of time at any time up to 12 weeks after practical completion (cl 2·19·3), and may review any extension of time previously given. The final review may extend the date previously fixed but may not bring it forward, although the contract administrator may be able to offset a reduction or omission of work against the effect of another delaying event. It is clear that, at this point, there is no requirement for notification by the contractor. There is no requirement to notify the contractor if it is decided that no further extension is due, but again it would be reasonable to do so.

Assessment

4.23   The contractor is entitled to extensions of time properly due under the contract and any failure on the part of the contract administrator to administer the provisions correctly would constitute a breach of contract on the part of the employer. On the other hand, the contract administrator has no power to grant extensions of time except as provided for in the contract, and for delays caused by relevant events as listed in clause 2·20.

4.24   The contract administrator should make an objective assessment of every notice received. The aim is to establish, if a delay has been caused by the event cited, whether the delay is likely to disrupt the programme and consequently delay the final completion date and, if so, to assess the probable extent of that final delay. The contractor's programme can be used as a guide and may be particularly useful where the programme shows a critical path but, although it may be persuasive evidence, it is not conclusive or binding. The effect on progress is assessed in relation to the work being carried out at the time of the delaying event, rather than the work that was programmed to be carried out.

4.25   It should be noted that the contract specifically states that certain events will *not* entitle the contractor to an extension of time, namely delays caused by the contractor's failure to comply with CDM Regulation 13, or by failure to provide design documents and related information within the stipulated timescales (cl 2·14·2). In addition, clause 2·19 contains the important proviso that the contractor must 'constantly use his best endeavours to prevent delay' (cl 2·19·4·1). The proviso refers to preventing delay caused by a relevant event, not to preventing the event itself. The contract administrator can assume, therefore, that the contractor will take steps to minimise the effect of the delay on the completion date, e.g. through reprogramming the remaining works. The phrase 'best endeavours' appears to suggest something more than 'reasonable' or 'practicable' but it is unlikely to extend to excessive expenditure. Clause 2·19·4·1 also states that the contractor 'shall do all that may reasonably be required to the satisfaction of the Architect/Contract Administrator to proceed with the Works'. However, if the contract administrator requires measures which amount to a variation, then this may result in a claim for loss and/or expense.

4.26   The effects of any delay on completion – taking into account the contractor's 'best endeavours' – are not always easy to predict. The contract administrator is required to reach an opinion, and in doing this the contract administrator owes a duty to both parties to be fair and reasonable. This applies even where the delay has been caused by the contract administrator, for example where the contract administrator has failed to issue drawings within the time limits stipulated in the contract.

4.27   It sometimes happens that two or more delaying events can happen simultaneously, or with some overlap, and this can raise difficult questions with respect to the awarding of extensions of time. In the case of concurrent delays involving two or more events (cl 2·20), it has been customary to grant the extension in respect of the dominant reason for the relevant event, but this is only appropriate where the dominant 'Relevant' reason begins before, and ends after, any other reasons. Even then, if the dominant reason is not a ground for loss and expense, this may still be due in respect of the other delaying events (*H Fairweather & Co.* v *Wandsworth*).

H Fairweather & Co. Ltd v *London Borough of Wandsworth* (1987) 39 BLR 106

Fairweather entered into a contract with the London Borough of Wandsworth to erect 478 dwellings. The contract was on JCT63. Pipe Conduits Ltd was the nominated sub-contractor for underground heating works. Disputes arose and an arbitrator was appointed who made an interim award. Leave to appeal was given on several questions of law arising out of the award. The arbitrator had found that, where a delay occurred which could be ascribed to more than one event, the extension should be granted for the dominant reason. Strikes were the dominant reason, and the arbitrator had therefore granted an extension of 81 weeks, and made it clear that this reason did not carry any right to claim for direct loss and/or expense. The court stated that an extension of time was not a condition precedent to an award of direct loss and/or expense, and that the contractor would be entitled to claim for direct loss and/or expense for other events which had contributed to the delay.

4.28   Where one overlapping delaying event is a clause 2·20 event and the other is not, in other words one is the employer's risk and the other the contractor's, a difficult question arises as to what extension of time is due. The instinctive reaction of many assessors might be to 'split the difference', given that both parties have contributed to the delay. However, the more logical approach is that the contractor should be given an extension of time for the full length of delay caused by the relevant event, irrespective of the fact that, during the overlap, the contractor was also causing delay. Taking any other approach, for example splitting the overlap period and awarding only half of the extension to the contractor, could result in the contractor being subject to liquidated damages for a delay partly caused by the employer. The courts have normally adopted this analysis (*Henry Boot Construction (UK) Limited v Malmaison Hotel*). More recently, in the much publicised Scottish case of *City Inn Ltd v Shepherd Construction Ltd*, the courts stated that a proportional approach would be fairer. This decision, however, is not binding on English courts and, at the time of writing, no cases in English courts have followed the proportionate approach, therefore the Malmaison approach remains the correct one to adopt.

Henry Boot Construction (UK) Ltd v Malmaison Hotel (Manchester) Ltd (1999) 70 Con LR 32 (TCC)

The employer, Malmaison, engaged Henry Boot to construct a new hotel in Piccadilly, Manchester. Completion was fixed for 21 November 1997, but was not achieved until 13 March 1998. However, extensions of time were issued by the architect revising the date for completion to 6 January 1998. Malmaison deducted liquidated damages from the contract sum. Although Henry Boot claimed further extensions of time in respect of a number of alleged relevant events, no further extensions of time were awarded. The case went to arbitration and the decision was challenged through court proceedings. Among other matters, the judge considered concurrency. If it can be shown that there are two equal and concurrent causes of delay, for which the employer and contractor are respectively responsible, then the contractor is still entitled to an extension of time. Judge Dyson illustrated his views on concurrency by citing the example of the start of a project being held up for one week by exceptionally inclement weather (a 'Relevant Event'), while at the same time the contractor suffered a shortage of labour (not a 'Relevant Event'). In effect, the two delays and causes were concurrent. In this situation, Judge Dyson said that the contractor should be awarded an extension of time of one week, and an architect should not deny the contractor an extension on the grounds that the project would have been delayed by the labour shortage.

City Inn Ltd v Shepherd Construction Ltd [2008] CILL 2537, Outer House Court of Session

In considering a case involving a dispute over extensions of time under a JCT80 form of contract, the court considered earlier authorities and the principles underlying extension of time clauses and set out several propositions. These included that, where there are several causes of delay and where a dominant cause can be identified, the assessor can use the dominant cause and set aside immaterial causes. However, where there are two causes of delay, only one of which is a contractor default, the assessor may apportion delay between the two events. The CILL editors describe this as going 'further than any recent authority' on concurrency. Assessors should note that this is a Scottish case which has not, to date, been followed in English courts.

Partial possession

4.29   The employer may take possession of completed parts of the works ahead of practical completion by operating clause 2·25. 'Partial possession' requires the agreement of the contractor, which cannot be unreasonably withheld. To bring the provision into operation the contract administrator must issue a written statement to the contractor identifying precisely the extent of the 'Relevant Part' and the date of possession (the 'Relevant Date'). This should be done with great care, even using a drawing to illustrate the extent, and communicating with the insurers where relevant. The statement must be issued immediately after the part is taken into possession, but in practice it would be wise to circulate the drawings and information in advance, so that all parties are clear as to the details of what will occur. The partial possession may affect other operations on site, in which case it could constitute an 'impediment', therefore the employer should be warned of the possible contractual consequences in terms of delay and claims for loss and/or expense.

4.30   Practical completion is 'deemed to have occurred' for the 'Relevant Part' of the works and the rectification period for that part is deemed to have commenced on the relevant date. The certificate of making good has to be issued for that part separately (cl 2·27). However, it would appear that this remains part of the works, and is still to be included under the certificate of practical completion. It is notable that the clause does not state that the works to that part must have reached practical completion, but in view of the contractual consequences it would be unwise for the employer to take possession before they have (see paragraph 4.37).

4.31   Liquidated damages are reduced by the proportion of the value of the 'Relevant Part' of the works to the contract sum and half of the retention is released for that proportion of the works. If Insurance Option C applies, the employer is responsible for insuring the possessed part under Schedule 1 paragraph C·1 (cl 2·28). If Insurance Option A or B applies, the employer may wish to consider insuring the part as the contractor's obligation to insure the works will cease.

4.32   It is important to note that the fact that significant work remains outstanding has not prevented the courts from finding that 'partial possession' has been taken of the whole works in situations where a tenant has effectively occupied the whole building, allowing access to the contractor for remedial work (see *Skanska Construction (Regions) Ltd* v *Anglo-Amsterdam Corporation Ltd*). If the parties do not intend clause 2·25 to take effect for the whole project, they must make clear, under a carefully worded agreement, what are the contractual consequences of any intended occupation (see below).

Skanska Construction (Regions) Ltd v *Anglo-Amsterdam Corporation Ltd* (2002) 84 Con LR 100

Anglo-Amsterdam Corporation (AA) engaged Skanksa Construction (Skanska) to construct a purpose-built office facility under a JCT81 With Contractor's Design form of contract. Clause 16 had been amended to state that practical completion would not be certified unless the certifier was satisfied that any unfinished works were 'very minimal and of a minor nature and not fundamental to the beneficial occupation of the building'. Clause 17 of the form stated that practical completion would be deemed to have occurred on the date that the employer took possession of 'any part or parts of the Works'.

AA wrote to Skanska confirming that the proposed tenant for the building would commence fitting-out works on the completion date. However, the air-conditioning system was not functioning and

Skanska had failed to produce operating and maintenance manuals. Following this date the tenant took over responsibility for security and insurance, and Skanska was allowed access to complete outstanding work. AA alleged that Skanska was late in the completion of the works and applied liquidated damages at the rate of £20,000 per week for a period of approximately nine weeks. Skanska argued that the building had achieved practical completion on time or that, alternatively, partial possession of the works had taken place and that, consequently, its liability to pay liquidated damages had ceased under clause 17.

The case went to arbitration and Skanska appealed. The court was unhappy with the decision and found that clause 17·1 could also operate when possession had been taken of all parts of the works and was not limited to possession of only part or some parts of the works. Accordingly, it found that partial possession of the entirety of the works had, in fact, been taken some two months earlier than the date of practical completion, when AA agreed to the tenant commencing fit-out works. Consequently, even though significant works remained outstanding, Skanska was entitled to repayment of the liquidated damages that had already been deducted by AA.

Use or occupation before practical completion

4.33   Situations can arise where the contractor has not completed by the date for completion and, although no sections of the works are sufficiently complete to allow the employer to take possession of those parts under clause 2·25, the employer is nevertheless anxious to occupy at least part of the works. There is nothing in the contract that allows for this. A suggestion was put forward in the 'Practice Section' of the *RIBA Journal* (February 1992) which has frequently proved useful in practice (see Figure 9): in return for being allowed to occupy the premises, the employer agrees not to claim liquidated damages during the period of occupation. Practical completion obviously cannot be certified, and there is no release of retention money until it is. Matters of insuring the works will need to be settled with the insurers.

4.34   Because such an arrangement would be outside the terms of the contract, it should be covered by a properly drafted agreement which is signed by both parties. (The cases of *Skanska* v *Anglo-Amsterdam Corporation* above and *Impresa Castelli* v *Cola* illustrate the importance of drafting a clear agreement.) It may also be sensible to agree that, in the event that the contractor still fails to achieve practical completion by the end of an agreed period, liquidated damages would begin to run again, possibly at a reduced rate. In most circumstances this arrangement would be of benefit to both parties, and is certainly preferable to issuing a heavily qualified practical completion certificate listing 'except for' items.

Impresa Castelli SpA v *Cola Holdings Ltd* (2002) CLJ 45

Impresa agreed to build a large four-star hotel for Cola Holdings Ltd (Cola), using the JCT Standard Form of Building Contract With Contractor's Design, 1981 edition. The contract provided that the works would be completed within 19 months from the date of possession. As the work progressed, it became clear that the completion date of February 1999 was not going to be met, and the parties agreed a new date for completion in May 1999 (with the bedrooms being made available to Cola in March) and a new liquidated damages provision of £10,000 per day, as opposed to the original rate

Figure 9 Practice Section, *RIBA Journal* (February 1992)

Contracts

Employer's possession before practical completion under JCT contracts

It is not uncommon for the employer after the completion date has passed to wish to take possession of the Works before the contractor has achieved practical completion. In this event an ad hoc agreement between employer and contractor is required to deal with the situation.

In respect of such an agreement members may wish to have regard to the following note …

Outstanding items

Where it is known to the architect that there are outstanding items, practical completion should not be certified without specially agreed arrangements between the employer and the contractor. For example, in the case of a contract where the contract completion date has passed it could be so agreed that the incomplete building will be taken over for occupation, subject to postponing the release of retention and the beginning of the defects liability period until the outstanding items referred to in a list to be prepared by the architect have been completed, but relieving the contractor from liability for liquidated damages for delay as from the date of occupation, and making any necessary changes in the insurance arrangements.

In such circumstances either the Certificate of Practical Completion form should not be used or it should be altered to state or refer to the specially agreed arrangements. In making such arrangements the architect should have the authority of the client-employer.

When the employer is pressing for premature practical completion there is a need to be particularly careful where there are others who are entitled to rely on the issue of a Practical Completion Certificate and its consequences. In the case where part only of the Works is ready for hand-over the partial possession provisions* can be operated to enable the employer with the consent of the contractor to take possession of the completed part.

*JCT80: clause 18
IFC84: clause 2·11 in appendix to JCT Practice Note IN11
(if incorporated in the contract)

of £5,000. Once the agreement was in place, further difficulties with progress were encountered, which meant that the May 1999 completion date was also unachievable. The parties entered into a second variation agreement, which recorded that access for Cola would be allowed to parts of the hotel to enable it to be fully operational by September 1999, despite certain works not being complete (including the air conditioning). In September 1999, parts of the hotel were handed over, but Cola claimed that such parts were not properly completed. A third variation agreement was put in place with a new date for practical completion and for the imposition of liquidated damages.

Disputes arose and, among other matters, Cola claimed for an entitlement for liquidated damages. Impresa argued that it had achieved partial possession of the greater part of the works, therefore a reduced rate of liquidated damages per day was due. The court found that, although each variation agreement could have used the words 'partial possession', they had in fact instead used the word 'access'. The court had to consider whether partial possession had occurred under clause 17·1 of the contract, which provides for deemed practical completion when partial possession is taken, or whether Cola's presence was merely 'use or occupation' under clause 23·3·2 of the contract. The court could find nothing in the variation agreements to suggest that partial possession had occurred. It therefore ruled that what had occurred related to use and occupation, as referred to in clause 23·3·2 of the contract, and that the agreed liquidated damages provision was therefore enforceable.

Practical completion

4.35	The contract administrator is obliged to certify practical completion of the works or of a section (cl 2·21·1) when, in the contract administrator's opinion, the following two criteria are fulfilled:

- practical completion of the works is achieved (see below);

- the contractor has sufficiently complied with clause 3·18·4 (supply of information required for the health and safety file).

In addition, in the case of ICD11 only, the contractor must have sufficiently complied with clause 2·32 (supply of as-built drawings).

4.36	Clause 2·21 then continues by stating that 'practical completion of the Works or the Section shall be deemed for all the purposes of this Contract to have taken place on the date stated in that certificate'. Although the wording of clause 2·21 is somewhat circular, effectively saying that 'Practical Completion of the Works or the Section' is to be certified when 'practical completion of the Works or the section' plus another event has taken place, it is suggested that a correct analysis of this clause is that practical completion only occurs when both conditions are met, the principal argument for this reasoning being that only one date is entered on the certificate. The contract administrator would be entitled to withhold the certificate until all significant health and safety information has been received, even if the actual works have been finished for some time, and would certainly be entitled to do so if the lack of information put the employer at risk of being in breach of the CDM Regulations. It should be noted that the contractor's obligation to supply information for the health and safety file depends on the CDM co-ordinator having requested it in writing (cl 3·18·4). Even then, the use of the term 'complied sufficiently' (cl 2·21) may allow the contract administrator to use its discretion in issuing the certificate despite some information being missing.

4.37	Deciding when the works have reached practical completion often causes some difficulty. It is suggested that practical completion means the completion of all works required under the contract and by subsequent instruction. Although it has been held that the contract administrator has discretion to certify practical completion where there are very minor items of work left incomplete, on *de minimis* principles (*H W Nevill (Sunblest)* v *William Press*), this discretion should be exercised with extreme caution. Contrary to the opinion of many contractors, there is no obligation to issue the certificate when the project is 'substantially' complete, or even when it is capable of occupation by the client, if there are items still outstanding.

H W Nevill (Sunblest) Ltd v *William Press & Son Ltd* (1981) 20 BLR 78

William Press entered into a contract with Sunblest to carry out foundations, groundworks and drainage for a new bakery on a JCT63 contract. A practical completion certificate was issued and new contractors commenced a separate contract to construct the bakery. A certificate of making good defects and a final certificate were then issued for the first contract, following which it was discovered that the drains and the hardstanding were defective. William Press returned to site and remedied the defects, but the second contract was delayed by four weeks and Sunblest suffered damages as a result. It commenced proceedings, claiming that William Press was in breach of contract and, in its defence, William Press argued that the plaintiff was precluded from bringing the claim by the conclusive effect of the final certificate. Judge Newey decided that the final certificate did not act as a bar to claims for consequential loss. In reaching this decision, he considered the meaning and effect of the certificate of practical completion and stated 'I think that the word "practically" in clause 15(1) gave the architect a discretion to certify that William Press had fulfilled its obligation under clause 21(1) where very minor *de minimis* work had not been carried out, but that if there were any patent defects in what William Press had done then the architect could not have issued a Certificate of Practical Completion' (at page 87).

4.38   The reason for proceeding with extreme caution is the considerable complications that can arise as a result of premature certification. Even though the employer, anxious to move into the newly completed works, may be pressing for early completion, and the contractor, anxious to avoid liquidated damages, may be even more enthusiastic, the temptation to issue the certificate, particularly one qualified by long schedules of outstanding work, should be resisted. The contract administrator should explain to the employer that they would be in a difficult position contractually, as the following contractual problems will remain unresolved:

- half of the retention will be released, leaving only half in hand (cl 4·8·1). This puts the employer at considerable risk, as the 2.5 per cent remaining from the 5 per cent stated in the Contract Particulars is only intended to cover latent defects;

- the rectification period begins (cl 2·30);

- the onus shifts to the contract administrator to notify the contractor of all necessary outstanding work under clause 2·30. If the contract administrator fails to include any item, the contractor would have no authority to enter the site to complete it – therefore the contract administrator will inevitably become involved in managing and programming the outstanding work;

- possession of the site now passes to the employer, and the contractor will no longer cover the insurance of the works;

- the contractor's liability for liquidated damages ends;

- interim certificates will be issued at two-monthly intervals (cl 4·7·1·3);

- the employer will be the 'occupier' for the purposes of the Occupiers' Liability Acts 1957 and 1984 and may also be subject to health and safety claims.

4.39   The certificate must be issued as soon as the criteria in clause 2·21 are met. The contractor is obliged to complete 'on or before' the completion date and once practical completion is certified the employer is obliged to accept the works. Employers who wish to accept the works only on the date given in the contract will need to amend the wording. If sectional completion is used, practical completion must be certified for each section of the works.

Procedure at practical completion

4.40   The contract sets out no procedural requirements for what must happen at practical completion, it simply requires the contract administrator to certify it. The contract bills may set out a procedure, and the contract administrator should check carefully at tender stage to ensure that the procedure is satisfactory.

4.41   Leading up to practical completion, it appears to be widespread practice for contract administrators to issue 'snagging' lists, sometimes in great detail and on a room-by-room basis. The contract does not require this, and neither do most standard terms of appointment. Under the contract, responsibility for quality control and snagging rests entirely with the contractor. In adopting this role, the contract administrator may be assisting the contractor and, although this may appear to benefit the employer, it may lead to confusion over the liability position, which could cause problems at a future date. If the contract administrator feels that the works are not complete, there is no obligation to justify this opinion with detailed schedules of outstanding items. It is suggested that the best course may be to draw attention to typical items, but to make it clear that the list is indicative and not comprehensive.

4.42   It is common practice for the contractor to arrange a 'handover' meeting. The term is not used in IC11 and, although handover meetings can be useful, particularly in introducing the finished project to the employer, the fact that one has been arranged or taken place is of no contractual significance. Even where a meeting has taken place at which the employer has expressed approval of the works, or the contractor has stated in writing that the works are complete, it remains the contract administrator's responsibility to decide when practical completion has been achieved.

Failure to complete by the completion date

4.43   In the event of failure to complete by the completion date, the contract administrator is required to certify this fact as a certificate of non-completion (cl 2·22). It should be noted that the issue of the certificate is an obligation on the contract administrator and not a matter of discretion. It should be issued promptly, as the certificate is a condition precedent to deduction of liquidated damages (cl 2·23). If the works are divided into sections, a separate certificate will be needed for each incomplete section. Once the certificate has been issued, the contractor is said to be in 'culpable delay'. The employer, provided that it has issued the necessary notices, may then deduct the damages from the next interim certificate, or reclaim the sum as a debt. Note that fluctuations provisions are frozen from this point. If a new completion date is later set, this has the effect of cancelling the certificate of non-completion and the contract administrator must issue a further certificate of non-completion if necessary.

Liquidated and ascertained damages

4.44   The agreed rate for liquidated and ascertained damages (LADs) is entered in the contract particulars. This is normally expressed as a specific sum per week (or other unit) of delay, to be allowed by the contractor in the event of failure to complete by the completion date (note that several different rates may apply where the works are divided into sections). The amount must be calculated on the basis of a genuine pre-estimate of the loss likely to be suffered (*Alfred McAlpine Capital Projects* v *Tilebox*). Provided that it is calculated on this basis, the sum will be recoverable without the need to prove the actual loss suffered, and irrespective of whether the actual loss is significantly less or more than the recoverable sum. In other words, once the rate has been agreed, both are bound by it. If 'nil' is inserted into the contract particulars then this may preclude the employer from claiming any damages at all (*Temloc* v *Errill*), whereas if no sum is entered the employer may be able to claim general damages.

Alfred McAlpine Capital Projects Ltd v *Tilebox Ltd* [2005] BLR 271

This case contains a useful summary of the law relating to the distinction between liquidated damages and penalties. A WCD98 contract contained a liquidated damages provision in the sum of £45,000 per week. On the facts, this was a genuine pre-estimate of loss and the actual loss suffered by the developer, Tilebox, was higher. The contractor therefore failed to obtain a declaration that the provision was a penalty. The judge also considered a different (hypothetical) interpretation of the facts whereby it was most unlikely, although just conceivable, that the total weekly loss would be as high as £45,000. In this situation also the judge considered that the provision would not constitute a penalty. In reaching this decision he took into account the fact that the amount of loss was difficult to predict, that the figure was a genuine attempt to estimate losses, that the figure was discussed at the time that the contract was formed and that the parties were, at that time, represented by lawyers.

Temloc Ltd v *Errill Properties* Ltd (1987) 39 BLR 30 (CA)

Temloc entered into a contract with Errill Properties to construct a development near Plymouth. The contract was on JCT80 and was in the value of £840,000. '£ nil' was entered in the contract particulars against clause 24·2, liquidated and ascertained damages. Practical completion was certified around six weeks later than the revised date for completion. Temloc brought a claim against Errill Properties for non-payment of some certified amounts, and Errill counterclaimed for damages for late completion. It was held by the court that the effect of '£ nil' was not that the clause should be disregarded (because, for example, it indicated that it had not been possible to assess a rate in advance), but that it had been agreed that no damages would be payable in the event of late completion. Clause 24 is an exhaustive remedy and covers all losses normally attributable to a failure to complete on time. The defendant could not, therefore, fall back on the common law remedy of general damages for breach of contract.

4.45   Before liquidated and ascertained damages may be claimed, the following preconditions must have been met:

• the contractor must have failed to complete the works by the date for completion or any extended date;

• the contract administrator must have issued a certificate of non-completion (cl 2·22);

• the contract administrator must have fulfilled all duties with respect to the award of an extension of time (cl 2·19·2);

• the employer must have given the contractor written notice of its intention before the date of the final certificate (cl 2·23·1·2).

4.46   The clause 2·23·1·2 notice must be reasonably clear, but there is no need for a great deal of detail (*Finnegan* v *Community Housing Association*). Provided these conditions have been met, the employer may, by means of a further notice 'no later than five days before the final date for payment of the amount payable under clause 4·14', recover the liquidated damages (cl 2·23·1). The notice to be given depends on whether the employer intends to deduct liquidated damages from monies due, or to require the contractor to pay the sum to the employer (cl 2·23·2). If the employer wishes to recover the amount as a debt then this has to be notified as set out in clause 2·23·2·1. If the employer wishes to deduct liquidated damages from an amount payable on a certificate, then a clause 2·23·2·2 notice is needed. In addition to this notice, footnote 39 (or 42 in ICD11) to clause 2·23·2·2 states that the employer must give the appropriate 'Pay Less Notice' under clause 4·11·5, 4·14·4 or 4·14·6·3 (this provision derives from the requirements of section 111 of the HGCRA 1996 Part II). Although the pay less notice may seem to be something of a duplication of the clause 2·32·2·2 notice, in that if correctly worded one document could cover both clauses, it would be wise to follow the footnote exactly and issue two separate notices complying precisely with the respective clauses.

J F Finnegan Ltd v *Community Housing Association Ltd* (1995) 77 BLR 22 (CA)

Finnegan Ltd was employed by the Housing Association to build 18 flats at Coram Street, West London. The contractor failed to complete the work on time, and the contract administrator issued a certificate of non-completion. Following the certificate of practical completion, an interim certificate was issued. The employer sent a notice with the cheque honouring the certificate, which gave minimal information (i.e. not indicating how LADs had been calculated). The Court of Appeal considered this sufficient to satisfy the requirement for the employer's written notice in clause 24·2·1. Peter Gibson LJ stated (at page 33):

I consider that there are only two matters which must be contained in the written requirement. One is whether the employer is claiming a payment or a deduction in respect of LADs. The other is whether the requirement relates to the whole or a part (and, if so, what part) of the sum for the LADs.

He then stated (at page 35):

I would be reluctant to import into this commercial agreement technical requirements which may be desirable but which are not required by the language of the clause and are not absolutely necessary.

The requirements relating to notices have now changed. However, there appears to be no reason why the general comments would not still apply, i.e. that the amount of information required would be no more than the minimum set out in the contractual provisions.

4.47   If an extension of time is given following the issue of a certificate of non-completion, then this has the effect of cancelling that certificate. A new certificate of non-completion must be issued if the contractor then fails to complete by the new completion date (cl 2·22). The employer must, if necessary, repay any liquidated damages recovered for the period up to the new completion date (cl 2·24), and must do so within a reasonable period of time (*Reinwood* v *L Brown & Sons*). Clause 2·23·3 also states that any notice issued by the employer under clause 2·23·1·2 shall remain effective, unless the employer states otherwise in writing, notwithstanding that a further extension of time has been granted. Nevertheless, it is suggested that, if the intention is to withhold payments due and the deduction was postponed to a later certificate, fresh notices should be issued.

Reinwood Ltd v *L Brown & Sons Ltd* [2007] BLR 305 (CA)

This dispute concerned a contract on JCT98, with a date for completion of 18 October 2004, and LADs at the rate of £13,000 per week. The project was delayed, and on 7 December 2005, the contractor made an application for an extension of time. On 14 December 2005, the contract administrator issued a certificate of non-completion under clause 24·1. On 11 January 2006, the contract administrator issued interim certificate no. 29 showing the net amount for payment as £187,988. The final date for payment was 25 January 2006.

On 17 January 2006, the employer issued notices under clause 24·2 and 30·1·1·3 of its intention to withhold £61,629 LADs, and the employer duly paid £126,359 on 20 January 2006.

On 23 January 2006, the contract administrator granted an extension of time until 10 January 2006, following which the contractor wrote to the employer stating that the effect of the extension of time and revision of the completion date was that the employer was now entitled to withhold no more than £12,326. The amount due under interim certificate no. 29 was, therefore, £175,662. Subsequently, the contractor determined the contract, relying partly on the late repayment of the balance by the employer.

The appeal was conducted on the issue of whether the cancellation of the certificate of non-completion by the grant of an extension of time meant that the employer could no longer justify a deduction of LADs. The employer's appeal was allowed. The judge stated that 'If the conditions for the deduction of LADs from a payment certificate are satisfied at the time when the employer gives notice of intention to deduct, then the Employer is entitled to deduct the amount of LADs specified in the notice, even if the certificate of non-completion is cancelled by the subsequent grant of an extension of time.' The employer must, however, repay the additional amount deducted within a reasonable time.

4.48   In *Department of Environment for Northern Ireland* v *Farrans* it was decided that the contractor has the right to interest on any repaid liquidated damages. This decision, however, was on JCT63 and, given that IC11 expressly refers to repayment without stipulating that interest is due, it would appear that interest would not be due in this situation. This was the view taken by His Honour Judge Carr in the first instance decision of *Finnegan* v *Community Housing Association* (1993) 65 BLR 103 (at page 114).

Department of Environment for Northern Ireland v *Farrans (Construction) Ltd* (1982) 19 BLR 1 (NI)

Farrans was employed to build an office block under JCT63. The original date for completion was 24 May 1975, but this was subsequently extended to 3 November 1977. During the course of the contract the architect issued four certificates of non-completion. By 18 July 1977, the employer had deducted £197,000 in liquidated damages but, following the second non-completion certificate, repaid £77,900 of those deductions. This process was repeated following the issue of the subsequent non-completion certificates. Farrans brought proceedings in the High Court of Justice in Northern Ireland, claiming interest on the sums that had subsequently been repaid. The court found for the contractor, stating that the employer had been in breach of contract in deducting monies on the basis of the first, second and third certificates, and that the contractor was entitled to interest as a result. The BLR commentary should be noted, which questions whether a deduction of liquidated damages empowered by clause 24·2 can be considered a breach of contract retrospectively. However, the case has not been overruled.

4.49   Certificates should always show the full amount due to the contractor. It is the employer alone who makes the deduction of liquidated damages. The employer would not be considered to have waived its claim by a failure to deduct damages from the first or any certificate under which this could validly be done, and would always be able to reclaim them as a debt at any point up until the final certificate.

5 Control of the works

5.1 The contract administrator's authority derives from the wording of the form. The contract places various duties on the contract administrator, for example to supply necessary information and to issue certificates or statements, and it also confers on the contract administrator a wide variety of powers, such as the power to issue instructions (see Figures 10 and 11). In some matters the contract administrator will act as agent of the employer, for example when issuing instructions which vary the works, and, in others, as an independent decision-maker, e.g. when deciding on claims for direct loss and/or expense. When making a decision between the parties, it would be implied that the contract administrator must act fairly at all times.

5.2 Failure by the contract administrator to comply with any obligation, either express or implied, may result in the contractor suffering losses. The contract administrator is not a party to the contract, therefore if the contractor wishes to bring a claim, this would, in the first instance, have to be against the employer. The contract administrator's obligations to the employer derive, of course, from the terms (either express or implied) of the professional appointment as agreed with the employer. It is likely, however, that any failure to administer the building contract according to its terms would be a breach of the contract administrator's

Figure 10 IC11/ICD11 Key powers of the contract administrator

2·9	instruct errors in setting out can remain
2·17	consent to removal of goods from site
2·30	instruct defects are not to be made good
3·5	consent to domestic sub-contractors
3·11·1	issue instructions requiring a variation
3·11·3/3·11·4	sanction a variation by the contractor
3·12	issue instructions postponing work
3·14 and 3·15	require contractor to open up work/get work tested
3·16·1	issue instructions requiring removal of work not in accordance with contract
3·16·2	issue instructions regarding work not carried out in a proper and workmanlike manner
3·17	exclude persons from the site
6·5·1	instruct 6·5·1 insurance is taken out
8·4·1	give contractor notice of default(s)
Schedule 2	issue instructions naming a person as sub-contractor

Figure 11 IC11 Key duties of the contract administrator

1·9	send copies of certificates to the employer and contractor at the same time
2·8·2·1	provide contractor with copies of contract documents
2·8·2·2	provide contractor with further copies of contract drawings and specification/schedules of work/contract bills
2·9	determine any levels that may be required
2·10	provide contractor with copies of information referred to in the information release schedule
2·11	provide contractor with such further drawings as are reasonably necessary and issue necessary instructions
2·13	issue instructions regarding errors, inconsistencies or divergences in contract documents
2·15·1	issue instructions regarding any discrepancies/divergencies discovered between contract documents and statutory requirements
2·19·1	give an extension of time (if contractor submits a notice and contract administrator considers completion date will be delayed, and delay caused by a relevant event)
2·21	certify practical completion
2·22	issue certificate(s) of non-completion
2·25	issue statement regarding partial possession
2·30	notify contractor of defects
2·31	issue certificate of making good
3·7 and Schedule 2	issue instructions with regard to named sub-contractors
3·10	comply with contractor's request for empowering provision
3·13	issue instructions regarding provisional sums
4·7	certify interim payments
4·7·1·2	certify interim payment on practical completion
4·14	issue final certificate
4·17	ascertain or instruct quantity surveyor to ascertain any amounts of direct loss and/or expense incurred
6·5·1	where required, instruct contractor to take out joint names insurance policy

duties to the employer, and therefore the employer may seek, in turn, to recover the losses from the contract administrator.

5.3   Direct control over the carrying out of the contract works, including the manner in which the works are undertaken, is solely the responsibility of the main contractor under the contract. The contract administrator will normally inspect the work at intervals. The duty to inspect arises not from IC11, which includes no express provision relating to inspection or monitoring of work by the contract administrator, but directly from the terms of appointment. Clearly, when the contract administrator is required under the contract to form an opinion on various matters, including the standard of work and materials prior to issuing a certificate, then it would be implied, even if not expressly set out in the terms of appointment, that some form of inspection must take place.

Person-in-charge

5.4 The contractor is required to keep a competent 'person-in-charge' on the site 'at all reasonable times' (cl 3·2). What would constitute 'reasonable' would depend on the nature and scale of the project, but as the JCT has chosen not to use the term 'at all times', as in SBC11, it would appear that something less than full-time presence would be acceptable. There is no requirement in the contract conditions to have the person named, but, as this person may receive any instructions given by the contract administrator and therefore acts as the contractor's agent, it would be good practice to establish the identity of the person in a pre-contract meeting, and make sure this is recorded in writing.

Clerk of works

5.5 The employer is entitled to employ an independent clerk of works whose duty is 'to act solely as inspector on behalf of the Employer under the Architect/Contract Administrator's directions' (cl 3·3). The presence of a clerk of works does not lessen the contract administrator's own duty in respect of site inspection (*Kensington Health Authority* v *Wettern*) and the contract administrator should not treat the clerk of works as an agent carrying out work on behalf of the contract administrator. Unlike SBC11, IC11 does not give the clerk of works any authority to issue directions, therefore the role is confined to inspection on behalf of the employer. It would be implied that the contractor should give the clerk of works reasonable access and facilities, but it might be sensible to make this clear in the tender documents, particularly if the clerk of works is to maintain a permanent presence on site.

Kensington and Chelsea and Westminster Area Health Authority v *Wettern Composites* (1984) 31 BLR 57

Wettern Composites was the sub-contractor for the supply and erection of pre-cast concrete mullions for an extension to the Westminster Hospital, on which the Health Authority had also engaged architects, engineers and a clerk of works. Tersons Ltd was the main contractor. The hospital was completed in 1965, and in 1976 it was discovered that there were considerable defects in the mullions. The Health Authority brought an action against the architects, engineers and sub-contractors, though the latter subsequently went into liquidation. Judgment was given for the Health Authority. The architects had failed to exercise reasonable skill and care in ensuring conformity of the works to the design. Although a clerk of works was employed, this did not lessen the architects' responsibility. However, the Health Authority was vicariously liable for the contributory negligence of its clerk of works, and the damages recoverable from the architects were accordingly reduced by 20 per cent.

CDM co-ordinator

5.6   The CDM co-ordinator's duties derive from the CDM Regulations, and it is the employer's obligation under the contract to ensure that the CDM co-ordinator complies with these (cl 3·18·1). It is the contractor's responsibility to develop the construction phase plan so that it complies with the CDM Regulations, and to ensure that the works are carried out in accordance with the plan. The CDM co-ordinator will monitor the development of the plan, but has no duty to inspect the works and would be very unlikely to visit the site unless some very unusual circumstance arises, such as the discovery of an unanticipated hazard. The main responsibility for ensuring correct health and safety measures are employed on site rests with the contractor, both under statute and under the express terms of the contract (cl 3·18).

Information to be provided by the contract administrator

5.7   One of the key duties of the contract administrator under a construction contract is to supply the contractor with sufficient information to construct the works in accordance with its terms. In an ideal world, the contractor should be supplied with every piece of information required at the very start of the project but, in practice, this ideal is rarely achieved. Even if the works have been fully specified, it is likely, for example, that information regarding assembly, location, detail dimensions, colours, etc. will be needed by the contractor throughout the project. In many cases it will not have been possible to prepare this in advance as detailed information regarding the site, or perhaps in relation to named sub-contractor design items, will not have been available. In addition, circumstances may result in the need for a variation and the provision of revised or entirely new information to the contractor. Supply of information will usually form part of the contract administrator's express or implied duties to the employer under the terms of appointment.

5.8   IC11 refers in three places to the contract administrator's obligation to provide information. These refer to: setting-out information (cl 2·9); 'information referred to in the Information Release Schedule' (cl 2·10); and 'such further drawings or details as are reasonably necessary to explain and amplify the Contract Drawings' (cl 2·11·1). Although none of the information is required to be released under a 'contract administrator's instruction', this is frequent practice – and wise, as it would enable the clause provisions to be brought into operation if necessary (see 'Contract administrator's instructions', paragraph 5.23 below). If any of the information supplied introduces changes or additions to the works, it must be covered by a contract administrator's instruction requiring a variation.

5.9   Under clause 2·9 the contract administrator is responsible for supplying sufficient 'accurately dimensioned drawings' and for determining levels to enable the contractor to set out the works. The contractor must, at no cost to the employer, 'amend any errors' that result from its own inaccurate setting out. Alternatively, the contract administrator, with the employer's consent, may instruct that the error remains, in which case 'an appropriate deduction shall be made from the Contract Sum' (cl 2·9). There is no suggestion in the conditions as to how this might be assessed. In practice, it will be a matter for negotiation, based on the anticipated losses to the employer through, for example, the resulting reduction in value of the property plus any costs in professional fees for redesign. The error and the deduction should first be discussed with the employer, and the agreed deduction should ensure adequate compensation.

5.10   Information shown on the information release schedule must be supplied at the stipulated date. Failure to provide the information covered by clause 2·10 causes delay, an event for which an extension of time may be granted (cl 2·20·6) and may give rise to a direct loss and/or expense claim where the failure causes such loss or expense (cl 4·18·4). It could also be grounds for termination, but only where such failure has led to the suspension of the carrying out of the whole of the works for a continuous period that is stated in the contract particulars – if not stated, the period is two months – (cl 8·9·2·2). The obligation is qualified by the proviso 'except to the extent that the Architect/Contract Administrator is prevented by an act or default of the Contractor or of any Contractor's Persons' (cl 2·10). An act or default of the contractor might include, for example, failure to provide design documents as required by the contract and which the contract administrator needs to finalise part of the design.

5.11   There is no mechanism whereby the contract administrator may unilaterally adjust the schedule following an extension of time, for example. Such adjustments will have to be negotiated and agreed by the parties, and it may be necessary to do this on a regular basis, keeping the contract administrator involved (the contract allows the employer and contractor to agree changes to the information release schedule under clause 2·10). Parties should tackle this co-operatively, and note that the contract states that such agreement should not be unreasonably withheld. For example, if variations have been issued that involve additional work and have resulted in an extension of time, or if work has been omitted and an earlier completion date fixed, then it would be reasonable for the schedule to be adjusted to reflect these circumstances. If the contractor refuses to agree to an adjustment, the document will become worthless with respect to assessing extensions of time.

5.12   With respect to information not shown on the schedule, or where a schedule is not used, the contract administrator is under an obligation to provide 'such further drawings or details as are reasonably necessary to explain and amplify the Contract Drawings and shall issue such instructions … as are necessary to enable the Contractor to carry out and complete the Works' (cl 2·11·1). It is suggested that this obligation would extend to both amplification of information in the contract documents and providing full information regarding any variation that is required to be carried out. The inclusion of the word 'reasonably' suggests that the contractor can be expected to obtain some detailed information, for example manufacturers' fixing information. The contract administrator should be careful, however, in respect of leaving decisions to the contractor, as it may not always be possible to hold the contractor responsible should a detail or fixing fail.

5.13   Under IC11 the information and instruction should be provided in sufficient time to allow the contractor to complete by the completion date or, if the contractor appears unlikely to complete by this date, at a date when 'having regard to the progress of the Works' it is reasonably necessary for the contractor to receive the information (cl 2·11·2). (It should be noted that the contract administrator may, however, have a more onerous obligation under its terms of engagement). There is no general requirement for the contractor to apply for information in writing, but if the contractor has 'reason to believe that the Architect/Contract Administrator is not aware' of when information may be needed, the contractor should advise the contract administrator (cl 2·11·3). In practice, such advice may frequently be in the form of a programme indicating dates when information is required. As above, failure to provide the information and instructions under clause 2·11·1 would constitute a relevant event under clause 2·20·6 and a relevant matter which may give rise to a direct loss and/ or expense claim under clause 4·18·4, and possible grounds for termination under clause 8·9·2·2.

5.14   Under IC11 there is no provision for other consultants to issue information direct to the contractor; this would have to be done through the contract administrator. Delay in supplying necessary drawings by other consultants would therefore have the effect under the contract of a delay on the part of the contract administrator, i.e. a delay for which the employer is responsible. An obligation to supply information on time would normally be implied into the terms of engagement of any consultant, if not expressly set out (*Royal Brompton Hospital* v *Frederick Alexander Hammond*).

Royal Brompton Hospital National Health Service Trust v *Frederick Alexander Hammond and others (No. 4)* [2000] BLR 75

The Royal Brompton Hospital (RBH) engaged Frederick Alexander Hammond to undertake a £19 million construction project on a JCT80 standard form of contract. The contractor successfully claimed against RBH, including for losses suffered due to delays. RBH commenced proceedings against 16 defendants, who were all members of the professional team. A trial date was fixed to deal with a number of different issues, all of which were settled except for one relating to the consulting M&E engineers, Austen Associates Ltd (AA). The issue was whether AA was obliged to provide co-ordination and builder's work information so as to ensure that RBH complied with clause 5·4 of the main contract. The court decided that AA was under a duty to use reasonable skill and care in ensuring that the drawings were provided in time to enable the contractor to prepare its installation drawings, and thus to carry out and complete the works in accordance with the contract conditions.

Information provided by the contractor or named sub-contractor

5.15   The contractor may be required to provide information in regard to CDM Regulations requirements and, in the case of ICD11, in relation to the completion of design for which the contractor is responsible, under the contractor's designed portion of the works. In relation to the CDM Regulations, the contractor as 'Principal Contractor' may be required by the CDM co-ordinator to provide information in relation to the health and safety file (cl 3·18·4). In addition, the contractor as a 'designer' under Regulation 13 of the CDM Regulations would have a statutory duty to provide information. This role is expressly acknowledged under clause 2·10·2. It should be noted, however, that IC11 does not contain express provisions for 'as-built' drawings. If these are needed, the specific requirement must be set out in the bills and specification.

5.16   ICD11, on the other hand, contains provisions regarding the submission of the developing design by the contractor, in addition to the obligations in relation to the CDM Regulations. This information is essential in order for the contract administrator and employer to monitor the development of the design and to integrate it with the rest of the works. The contractor must provide two copies of: 'such Contractor's Design Documents and (if requested) related calculations and information, as are reasonably necessary to explain or to amplify the Contractor's Proposals'; and 'all levels and setting out dimensions which the Contractor prepares or uses for the purposes of carrying out and completing the Contractor's Designed Portion' (cl 2·10·2).

5.17   'Contractor's Design Documents' are defined as 'the drawings, details and specification of materials, goods and workmanship and other related documents prepared by or for the Contractor in relation to the Contractor's Designed Portion' (cl 1·1). The clause 2·10·2 information is to be provided 'as and when necessary from time to time in accordance with any design submission procedures set out in the Contract Documents', and 'the Contractor shall not commence any work to which such a document relates before that procedure has been complied with' (cl 2·10·3). The contractor is not entitled to any extension of time for delays caused by failure to supply this information, including failure to comply with a written request from the contract administrator specifying a date by which it is reasonably necessary to receive relevant information (cl 2·14·2).

5.18   In practice, there could be differences of opinion as to what information may be 'reasonably necessary'. The information that the contractor may need to actually construct the work may differ from the information that the employer and contract administrator would like to receive. Differences could also arise regarding the appropriate timing of submission of this information. Clause 2·10·3 therefore anticipates that the employer will wish to set out its own particular requirements for submissions. It would be open to the employer, and on most projects would be wise, to include detailed requirements regarding scope, format and timing of submissions in the contract documents.

5.19   There are no provisions to deal with any comments that the contract administrator might make on the information. Although this does not prevent the contract administrator from commenting, the contractor would not be obliged to incorporate the comments unless they took the form of an instruction varying the employer's requirements (cl 3·11·3). If the contractor does alter its design as a result of comments, the liability for the changed design is unclear. If the design is a significant part of the project and likely to be subject to comment, the parties might wish to agree a formal procedure. The system set out in Schedule 1 to SBC11 could be used as a model.

Information provided by the named sub-contractor

5.20   If ICSub/NAM/E is executed, the named sub-contractor will have an obligation to provide information to the contract administrator in accordance with any time requirements set out in Schedule 1 of the ICSub/NAM/E contract particulars or separate document to the form (cl 1). This information is stated under clause 1·1 to be for the purposes of either co-ordinating the design with that of the main contract (cl 1·1·1), obtaining the main contract tenders or instructing the expenditure of a provisional sum relating to the named sub-contractor (cl 1·1·2), or to enable the contract administrator to issue information to either the main contractor or the specialist (cl 1·1·3). The clause also requires the named sub-contractor to supply 'such further information as the Contract Administrator' may reasonably require. As discussed above, it would be wise to set out in Schedule 1 as much detail as possible about the type of information and timing of submission, to avoid any disagreements later as to what it might be reasonable to require.

5.21   The sub-contractor would be directly liable to the employer for any breach of the obligation to provide information, and the employer would therefore be able to bring a claim against the named sub-contractor for any losses suffered. It is notable that there are no terms in the main contract which expressly relieve the main contractor of liability, but as there are no terms requiring the contractor to provide information, it is very unlikely that the employer could claim losses from the main contractor. Any risk of late named sub-contractor information holding up progress would be borne by the employer through the operation of the extension of time and disruption provisions.

5.22   This named sub-contractor's obligation to provide information is subject to the employer providing information according to any dates agreed under Schedule 1 to ICSub/NAM/E or as may reasonably be required (cl 1·3). This means that, if the information is not provided according to the Schedule 1 dates, the employer will not be able to bring any claim against the named sub-contractor for losses suffered. If calendar dates are agreed, there are no means of adjusting them should the main contractor's (and consequently the sub-contractor's) programme be delayed. In practice, therefore, it may be better to relate those dates to work stages rather than calendar dates.

Contract administrator's instructions

5.23   Only the contract administrator has the power to issue instructions. Sometimes the contract administrator 'may' issue instructions (e.g. instructions requiring a variation under clause 3·11) but at other times the contract administrator 'shall' issue instructions (e.g. instructions regarding discrepancies between contract documents under clause 2·13). The latter is an obligation. If the employer gives an instruction other than through the contract administrator this would not be effective under the contract. The contractor would be under no obligation to comply with any such instruction. If the contractor, however, does carry out the instruction, a court might decide either that there had been an agreed amendment to the contract, or that the instructed work is not part of the contract but a separate agreement between the contractor and the employer. The consequences of such an agreement would be difficult to resolve in practice and the employer would be very unwise to make such agreements or issue any instructions other than through the contract administrator.

5.24   Where the contract administrator acts outside its authority, the contractor would be under no obligation to comply with the instruction given. On the other hand, provided that the contract administrator is acting within the terms of the contract, the contractor must comply, even if the contract administrator's action is contrary to the express requirements or instructions of the employer.

5.25   Instructions requiring a variation must be in writing (cl 1·7·1). The provisions make no reference to oral instructions, which would therefore be of no effect. The contractor would not be obliged to comply with any oral instruction and would be wise to request all instructions to be confirmed immediately in writing before taking action. If the contractor carries out a variation on the basis of an oral instruction only, then the contract administrator could later sanction the instruction in writing (cl 3·11) but the contractor would have taken a risk (*MOD* v *Scott Wilson Kirkpatrick*). The contract contains no provisions to cover the situation where the contractor confirms an oral instruction in writing; however, it might be wise to respond promptly, reminding the contractor of the correct procedures under the contract.

Ministry of Defence v *Scott Wilson Kirkpatrick* [2000] BLR 20 (CA)

Scott Wilson Kirkpatrick (SWK) was engaged as structural engineer and supervising officer by the MOD in relation to refurbishment of the roof at Plymouth Dockyard under GC/Works/1. Several years after the works were complete, wind lifted a large section of roof and deposited it in a nearby playing field. The contract had required 9–12in. nails, but the contractor had used 4in. nails. The supervising officer had been party to discussions regarding the use of the 4in. nails, but neither he nor the contractor could remember very clearly when these discussions happened, or exactly what had been said. The Court of Appeal decided the evidence was sparse and vague, and declined to find that there was any instruction under 7(1)(a) or 7(1)(m) (instructions that may be given orally), or that there had been any agreement as to the replacement. Even if the supervising officer's conduct amounted to confirmation or encouragement, this could not absolve the contractor from its duty to fix the purlins in a workmanlike manner. The MOD was therefore entitled to insist on its strict contractual rights. The Court of Appeal noted, however, that an instruction in writing was not a condition precedent to a claim by the contractor, so long as it was able to prove that the change had been agreed.

5.26   All instructions must be given to the contractor, or the contractor's agent on site, even if the instructions relate to named a sub-contractor's work. Instructions sent by fax or email would also be valid (see paragraph 9.8). In all cases, though, it should be remembered that it may be necessary to prove that an instruction has been received, and therefore sensible to send a hard copy by recorded delivery, or to record its receipt at a subsequent progress meeting. No special format is required for instructions, but it is good practice to have a system of numbered instructions in a standard format, and it is often convenient to use the forms published by RIBA Publishing. An instruction in a letter would nevertheless be effective, even if the normal practice on that project was to use the printed forms, as long as the letter is quite clear. A drawing sent with a letter requiring it to be executed would constitute an instruction, but a drawing with no covering instruction may be ineffective.

5.27   Instructions in site meeting minutes may constitute a written instruction if issued by the contract administrator, but not if issued by the contractor, and only if the minutes are recorded as agreed at a subsequent meeting. It is possible that the instruction would not take effect until after the minutes were agreed, and it would depend on the circumstances whether the minutes were sufficiently clear to fall within the terms of the contract. It is therefore not good practice to rely on this method. Site instruction books should also be avoided. Signing an instruction in a book would constitute a written instruction under the terms of the contract, but there is no obligation to sign such books, and it may be prudent not to make quick decisions on site but to wait until all implications can be checked. With the possibility of faxed instructions the delay should be very short.

5.28   The contractor must comply with every instruction (see Figure 12) provided that it is valid, i.e. provided that it is in respect of a matter regarding which the contract administrator is

Figure 12 Key matters about which the contract administrator is empowered to issue instructions

2·9	setting out
2·13	errors or inconsistencies
2·15·2	statutory requirements
2·30	making good defects
3·11	variations
3·12	postponement
3·13	expenditure of provisional sums
3·14	opening up and tests
3·16·1	removal of defective work
3·16·2	work not carried out in a proper and workmanlike manner
Schedule 2	named person as sub-contractors

empowered to issue instructions (cl 3·8). The contractor must 'forthwith' comply, which for practical purposes means as soon as is reasonably possible. There are two exceptions to this obligation; the contractor need not comply with a clause 5·1·2 instruction (access and use of the site, etc.) to the extent that it makes a reasonable objection (cl 3·8, or 3·8·1 in ICD11), and the contractor need not comply where it believes that the instruction 'injuriously affects the efficacy' of the contractor's design (cl 3·8·2, ICD only, see paragraph 5.37).

5.29   If the contractor feels that a contract administrator's instruction might not be empowered by the contract, or requires clarification, then the contractor may ask the contract administrator to specify in writing the provisions of the contract under which the instruction is given, and the contract administrator must do this 'forthwith' (cl 3·10). (To avoid this happening, it is good practice always to name the clause under which the instruction is empowered.) The contractor must then either comply or issue a notice referring the disputed instruction to the decision of an adjudicator. If, however, the contractor chooses to accept the contract administrator's reply and complies with the instruction, then the employer is bound by the instruction. This would appear to be the case even if it is established at a later stage that the contract administrator had no authority under the contract.

5.30   Even if the contractor decides to query the instruction under clause 3·10, this does not relieve the contractor of the obligation to comply. Should the instruction be found to be valid, the contractor would be liable for any delay caused by failing to comply as required by the contract. If the contractor does comply, but the instruction turns out to have been invalid, the contractor may be entitled to any losses incurred through compliance. The contractor would have to make a commercial decision regarding whether to comply or await the outcome, but the contract administrator would be wise to deal promptly with any such query.

5.31   If the contractor does not comply with a written instruction, the employer may employ and
pay others to carry out the work to the extent necessary to give effect to the instruction
(cl 3·9). The contract administrator must have given written notice to the contractor
requiring compliance with the instruction, and seven days must have elapsed after the
contractor's receipt of the notice before the employer may bring in others. This suggests
that some recorded form of delivery is desirable. Although there is no obligation to issue
such notices, it would be prudent to take swift action in order to protect the employer's
interests. The employer is entitled to recover any additional costs from the contractor, i.e.
the difference between what would have been paid to the contractor for the
instructed work and the costs actually incurred by the employer (the amount is deducted
from the contract sum; cl 4·8·3). These costs could include not only the carrying out of the
instructed work but any special site provisions that would need to be made, including
health and safety provisions, and any additional professional fees charged. Although it
would be wise to obtain alternative estimates for all these costs wherever possible, if the
work is needed urgently there would be no need to do so.

Variations

5.32   Contract administrators' instructions often require some variation to the works. Under
common law neither party to a contract has the power unilaterally to alter any of its terms.
Therefore, in a construction contract neither the employer nor the contract administrator
would have the power to require any variations unless the contract contains such a power.
As some aspects of construction may be difficult to define exactly in advance, most
construction contracts contain provisions allowing the employer to vary the works to some
degree. Changes can arise because of unexpected site problems, or because of design
changes required by the employer, or because the contract administrator has to change
information issued to the contractor.

5.33   Under IC11 the contract administrator is empowered to order specific variations (cl 3·11·1).
The power is broadly defined and includes alterations to the design, quality and quantity
of the works, and to operational restrictions such as access to the site. The contract
expressly states that no variation will vitiate the contract (cl 3·11·4, or 3·11·5 in ICD11) but
the power does not extend to altering the nature of the contract, nor can the contract
administrator issue variations after practical completion. All variations under clause 3·11
may result in an adjustment of the contract sum (cl 4·3·1·1) and give rise to a claim for an
extension of time (cl 2·20·1), or for direct loss and/or expense (cl 4·18·1). If the works are
suspended for a period of two months, or any period stated in the contract particulars, as
a consequence of the variation, this would be grounds for the contractor to terminate its
employment under the contract, unless the variation was necessitated by some negligence
or default of the contractor (cl 8·9·2).

5.34   The contract administrator may vary the works, e.g. by changing the standard of a material
specified. The contract administrator may add to or omit work, or substitute one type of
work for another or remove work already carried out (cl 3·11 and 5·1·1). The contract
administrator may vary the access to or use of the site, limitations on working space or
working hours, the order in which the work is to be carried out, or any restrictions already
imposed (cl 3·11 and 5·1·2) (SMM7 requires these to be set out separately). However, with
respect to clause 5·1·2 variations, the contractor need not comply to the extent that it

makes reasonable objection (cl 3·8). Given that the contractor will be paid for such variations it is difficult to see what might constitute a 'reasonable' objection, but, for example, a variation might have a detrimental knock-on effect on some other project, causing the contractor to suffer losses for which it would not otherwise be compensated or might involve an instruction that would make site operations almost impossible to manage. This contract provision is necessary not only to allow the employer some flexibility, but also to accommodate difficulties that may arise, for example through local authority restrictions on working hours.

5.35   The contract administrator may issue an instruction to postpone work (cl 3·12). Any such instruction may give rise to a claim for an extension of time (cl 2·20·1) or direct loss and/ or expense (cl 4·18·1), and if the postponement results in a suspension of work for a period greater than that stated in the contract particulars, then the contractor would have grounds for terminating its employment. The consequences of such an instruction are therefore serious, and the contract administrator would advise any client who is suggesting such a measure accordingly. It is difficult to envisage a situation where it would be necessary to postpone work, but it could arise where there have been problems with regard to statutory approval, or in reaching agreement over a boundary matter, and the only option might be to postpone the relevant part of the works.

5.36   Finally, the contract administrator may sanction any variation made by the contractor other than under an instruction of the contract administrator (cl 3·11·3). If such a variation were likely to affect the employer, the contract administrator would be wise to discuss it with the employer before taking action.

Variations to the contractor's designed portion

5.37   Clause 3·11·3 (ICD only) states that where an instruction requires a variation in respect of the contractor's designed portion, it shall be 'an alteration to or modification of the Employer's Requirements'. This would appear to prevent the contract administrator from requiring changes to the proposals after the contract is entered into, including to any further design details that are developed as the contract progresses, except in the case where the developing design does not meet the employer's requirements. If the contract administrator issues any instruction which, in the contractor's opinion, may affect the efficacy of the design, the contractor must object within seven days of receiving the instruction, specifying the injurious effect (cl 3·8·2). The instruction will not then take effect until confirmed by the contract administrator.

Goods, materials and workmanship

5.38   Clause 2·1 makes it clear that all work must be carried out in accordance with the standard specified in the contract documents. The contract administrator will normally inspect at regular intervals to monitor the standard that is being achieved. If any changes were made in order to raise or lower the standard then this would constitute variation. When the standard achieved appears to be unsatisfactory, it can be tempting to become involved in directing the day-to-day activities of the contractor on site. Apart from being an enormous burden on the contract administrator, this could confuse the issue of who is ultimately responsible for quality and is to be avoided. The contract administrator would normally, of course, draw the contractor's attention to areas of defective or poor quality work. There are also some measures set out in the contract, as detailed in the following section.

Defective work

5.39   The contract administrator may instruct the contractor to open up completed work for inspection, or arrange for testing of any of the work or materials, fixed or unfixed (cl 3·14). Obviously, the contract administrator would only do this if there are reasonable grounds for suspecting defective work or materials. No time limit is specified, but the contract administrator should instruct as soon as the need for such action becomes apparent (delay could result in escalating or unnecessary costs). Failure to ask for tests, however, in no way relieves the contractor from the obligation to provide work according to the contract. The contract administrator should explain to the employer the need for the tests and their contractual implications. The cost of carrying out the tests is added to the contract sum, unless it was already provided for in the bills of quantities under a provisional sum, or unless the work proves to be defective. Unless the work is defective the contractor may also be entitled to an extension of time under clause 2·20·2·3 and loss and/or expense under clause 4·18·2·3.

5.40   If work is found to be defective, the contractor must write to the contract administrator proposing action to be taken immediately to establish whether there are any similar problems in work already carried out. If the contract administrator has not received proposals within seven days, or is not satisfied with the contractor's proposals, or cannot wait seven days to receive the proposals, the contract administrator can instruct that further tests or opening up be carried out (cl 3·15·1). In this case the cost of further tests would be borne by the contractor, whether or not the additional tests demonstrated work to be defective. The contractor has a right of objection, which must be made within ten days of receipt of the instruction (cl 3·15·2) but, whether or not it exercises this right, it must comply with the instruction immediately. Following the objection, the contract administrator may either withdraw the instruction or modify it – if neither is done within seven days of the objection, and the matter cannot be resolved, it is referred to one of the contractual dispute resolution procedures (cl 3·15·2).

5.41   The contract administrator has the power to issue an instruction requiring the removal of work, materials or goods from the site (cl 3·16·1). Even though this might appear rather excessive considering that the contractor is already under an obligation to build the work correctly, it can be important to issue such instructions as they enable the clause 3·9 sanctions to be brought into operation (*Bath and NE Somerset DC* v *Mowlem*). To fall under clause 3·16·1, the instruction must specifically require removal of the work from site, however impractical. Simply drawing attention to the defective work would not be sufficient (*Holland Hannen* v *Welsh Health Technical Services*).

Bath and North East Somerset District Council v Mowlem plc [2004] BLR 153 (CA)

Mowlem plc was engaged on JCT98 (Local Authorities With Quantities) to undertake the Bath Spa project. Completion was expected to be in 2002 but work was still underway in 2003. Paint applied by Mowlem to the four pools began to peel, and the contract administrator issued architect's instruction no. 103 which required Mowlem to strip and repaint the affected areas. Mowlem refused to comply and the Council issued a notice under clause 4·1·2. Mowlem still did not comply, and the employer engaged Warings to carry out this work. Mowlem refused Warings access to the site, and the Council applied to the court for an injunction, which was granted. Mowlem appealed against the injunction, but the appeal was dismissed.

Mowlem had argued that it was able to rectify all the defects and that the liquidated damages provided under the contract were the agreed remedy for delays caused. The Council was able to show that the liquidated damages were not adequate compensation for the losses suffered. Lord Justice Mance held that, in such cases, the court should examine whether the liquidated damages would provide adequate compensation and, if they would not, as in this case, it is appropriate to grant an injunction. In reaching this decision he took into account irrecoverable losses such as the 'unquantifiable and uncompensatable damage to the Council's general public aims'.

Holland Hannen & Cubitts (Northern) Ltd v *Welsh Health Technical Services Organisation* (1985) 35 BLR 1 (CA)

Cubitts Ltd was employed by the Welsh Health Technical Services Organisation (WHTSO) to construct two hospitals at Rhyl and Gurnos. Percy Thomas (PTP) was the architect. Redpath Dorman Long Ltd (RDL) was the nominated sub-contractor for the design and supply of pre-cast concrete floor slabs. RDL assured WHTSO that the floors would be designed to CP 116 (concerning deflection), but the design team later required RDL to work to CP 204. Following installation, the contractor complained about extra work and costs due to adjustments to the partitions necessitated by excessive deflection of the floors, and it was established that they had been designed to CP 116 not CP 204. PTP sent three letters 'condemning' the floors, but the first did not mention clause 6(4), and none of them required removal of the work. Cubitts stopped work for 20 weeks until PTP issued instructions specifying how the defect should be resolved. Cubitts commenced proceedings claiming compensation for delay. The claim was settled, but the relevant parties maintained their proceedings against each other for contribution. The Official Referee decided that RDL was liable for two-thirds of the amount paid to Cubitts and the design team for one-third. The Court of Appeal decided that this was incorrect and the correct apportionment should have been that RDL was liable for one-third and the design team for two-thirds. In reaching this conclusion it stated: 'PTP contributed very substantially to the delay which occurred, in failing to recognise the defect in the design at an earlier stage; by issuing an invalid notice in 1976, and by moving very slowly thereafter to take the necessary steps to have the defects in the flooring put right' (Robert Goff LJ).

5.42   There are no express provisions in IC11 whereby the defective work, materials or goods can be allowed to remain – if this is required it would need to be covered by an instruction authorising a variation. It is essential to secure the employer's consent and agree a reasonable reduction in the contract sum with both parties. The contract administrator must specify in writing exactly which work may remain and record the agreed deduction. If variations to other work become necessary as a consequence it should be agreed (again following consultation with the employer and contractor) that no addition is made to the contract sum and no extension of time or direct loss and/or expense is given in respect of these subsequent variations. The contract administrator should strongly advise the employer against accepting any defective work that could later cause technical problems or be a source of irritation. The difficult case of *Ruxley Electronics* v *Forsyth* illustrates that it may not be possible to claim the cost of having the work rebuilt at a later date.

Ruxley Electronics and Construction Ltd v *Forsyth* (1995) 73 BLR 1 (HL)

Mr Forsyth employed Ruxley Electronics to build a swimming pool. The drawings and specification required the pool to be 7ft 6in. deep at its deepest point, but the completed pool was only 6ft 9in. deep. The contractors brought a claim for their unpaid account and Mr Forsyth counterclaimed the cost of rebuilding the pool, which would be £21,560. The trial judge found that the shortfall in depth did not decrease the value of the pool and that Mr Forsyth had no intention of building a new pool. He rejected the counterclaim but awarded £2,500 as general damages for loss of pleasure and amenity. Mr Forsyth appealed and the Court of Appeal allowed the appeal and awarded him £21,500. The contractor appealed and the House of Lords restored the original ruling, confirming that the cost of reinstatement is not the only possible measure of damages for defective performance of a building contract and is not the appropriate measure where the expenditure would be out of all proportion to the benefit to be obtained.

5.43   Clause 2·1 requires the contractor to carry out the work 'in a proper and workmanlike manner' and in accordance with the construction phase plan. Clause 3·16·2 states that, in the event of any failure, the contract administrator may issue instructions requiring compliance, and these will not result in any addition to the contract sum, nor will they entitle the contractor to any extension of time or direct loss and/or expense. The clause empowers the contract administrator to intervene in the contractor's working methods if necessary.

Sub-contracted work

5.44   IC11 provides for two methods of sub-contracting work, both allowing for some control over which firms the contractor uses.

Domestic sub-contractors

5.45   Under clause 3·5 the contractor may only sub-contract work (including CDP work) with the written consent of the contract administrator. Failure to obtain this would be a default, providing grounds for termination under clause 8·4·1·4. Clause 3·5 states, however, that the contract administrator's permission cannot be unreasonably withheld. It is suggested that permission is required for each instance of sub-letting, rather than agreeing to sub-letting in principle.

5.46   As discussed in paragraph 2.27, the JCT publishes a suite of sub-contract forms for use with domestic sub-contracts, including situations where the sub-contractor is to undertake design, but neither IC11 nor ICD11 requires that any particular form is used. Whatever form of domestic sub-contract is used, however, it must include certain conditions, and clause 3·6 states the sub-contract must provide that:

- the sub-contractor's employment is terminated immediately upon termination of the contractor's (cl 3·6·1);

- unfixed materials and goods placed on the site by the sub-contractor shall not be removed without written consent by the contractor (cl 3·6·2·1);

- it shall be accepted that materials or goods included in an interim certificate that has been paid by the employer become the property of the employer (cl 3·6·2·1·1);

- it shall be accepted that any materials or goods paid for by the contractor prior to being included in a certificate become the property of the contractor (cl 3·6·2·1·2);

- the sub-contractor will provide access to work as required by clause 3·1 (cl 3·6·2)

- the sub-contractor has a right to interest on late payments by the contractor at the same rate as that due on main contract payments (cl 3·6·4).

5.47   These clauses protect the position of the employer, and the provisions regarding unfixed goods and materials are of particular importance in this respect. If a main contractor should sub-contract on other terms, and this results in losses to the employer, then the contractor may be liable as this would be a breach of contract.

Named persons as domestic sub-contractors

5.48   The provisions for naming of sub-contractors are set out in clause 3·7 and Schedule 2. The sub-contractor can either be named in the contract bills/specification/work schedules, in which case the firm must have been selected prior to tendering the main contract, or in an instruction regarding a provisional sum. The latter route gives more flexibility to the employer but requires the employer to accept more risk.

5.49   Where the sub-contractor is named in the tender documents, the contractor must be provided at the time of tender with ICSub/NAM with the first two sections (ICSub/NAM/IT and ICSub/NAM/T) completed, documents referred to as 'the Tender Documents' that describe the work, which might include, for example, drawings and bills of quantities or specifications, together with a copy of the construction phase plan (if and to the extent available), and a copy of the executed ICSub/NAM/E. (A deed might be preferable where design work is involved, but there should be consistency between all documents.) Where the sub-contractor is named in an instruction relating to a provisional sum, the same information must accompany the instruction.

5.50   In order to collate this information, the contract administrator must first invite sub-contract tenders using ICSub/NAM. Included is the invitation to tender (ICSub/NAM/IT), to be completed and signed by the contract administrator, before it is sent to the invited sub-contractor. ICSub/NAM/IT contains such important items as the 'dates between which it is expected that the sub-contract work will be carried out', insurance and VAT arrangements and dispute resolution matters. If ICSub/NAM/E is being used this should be completed and sent at the same time. The sub-contractor then completes ICSub/NAM/T and ICSub/NAM/E (in part – detailed guidance notes are given in the form), and returns both to the contract administrator. If the offer is acceptable, the employer executes ICSub/NAM/E, which then forms a binding agreement.

5.51   There is an alternative procedure for use in situations where insufficient information is available to request a firm tender for the works, but the employer wishes to enter into a warranty. ICSub/NAM/E can be sent on its own (in this case with the appropriate part of the fourth recital deleted, or fifth recital in ICD11) and the sub-contractor submits an approximate estimate for the works. The warranty is executed on this basis, and a firm tender sought on ICSub/NAM/E when more information is available.

5.52   Where the sub-contractor is named in the main contract documents, the contractor will price this work when submitting its tender. The contractor must then enter into an agreement with the named person within 21 days of entering into the main contract with the employer. The agreement is made using the third section of ICSub/NAM/T, which refers to the sub-contract conditions ICSub/NAM/C (cl 3·7 and Schedule 2) (ICSub/NAM/C itself does not have to be executed). If the contractor is unable to enter into a sub-contract in accordance with the particulars in the main contract documents, the contractor must immediately inform the contract administrator of the particulars that have prevented this from happening (Schedule 2:2). The contract administrator must then issue an instruction which could either 'change the particulars so as to remove the impediment' (Schedule 2:2·1), or omit the work, substituting a provisional sum if wished (Schedule 2:2·3). It is suggested that, with the exception of cases where a named sub-contractor's employment has been terminated, the main contractor could not be required to carry out work which the tender documents stated were to be undertaken by a named (or to be named) sub-contractor.

5.53   An instruction under Schedule 2 paragraphs 2·1 and 2·2 is to be treated as a variation under clause 3·11, which may give rise to a claim for an extension of time, and also be a matter with respect to a claim for direct loss and/or expense (although this would be unlikely where the work is omitted). An instruction under Schedule 2 paragraph 2·3 is dealt with in accordance with Schedule 2 paragraph 5, i.e. as an instruction relating to a provisional sum, and therefore could also give rise to an adjustment of the contract sum, and an award of an extension of time or direct loss and/or expense. In addition, as with any instructions, if the contract administrator does not issue the necessary instructions promptly, this could give rise to claims under clauses 2·20·6 and 4·18·4 (delay or disruption due to failure to issue necessary instructions) and, where the works are suspended by two months or a period stated in the contract particulars as a consequence, to termination by the contractor. It is suggested that this would only apply where the contract administrator has failed to act within a reasonable time (*Percy Bilton Ltd* v *Greater London Council*). It is clear, however, that the risk of a problem arising while finalising the sub-contract details is borne in part by the employer, and it may be prudent for the contract administrator to check before the main contract tender is accepted that there appear to be no outstanding matters to be resolved before the sub-contract can be formed, particularly in cases where a considerable period has elapsed since the named person's tender was sought.

Percy Bilton Ltd v *Greater London Council* (1982) 20 BLR 1 (HL)

Percy Bilton Ltd contracted with the Greater London Council (GLC) for the provision of 182 dwellings. W J Lowdell Ltd was nominated to carry out mechanical services but, after commencing the work, withdrew its labour and went into liquidation. A second firm was then nominated, but this company withdrew its tender. Finally, a third firm was nominated and a sub-contract was entered into. The contractor claimed an extension of time which was only granted in part, and the contractor then brought proceedings for the return of liquidated damages that had been deducted. The GLC claimed that the problems of renomination were covered in clause 23(g) (delay on the part of a nominated sub-contractor) and therefore the extension of time and the deduction of liquidated damages was valid. Percy Bilton claimed that clause 23(g) did not cover that situation, which amounted to a breach on the part of the employer. The House of Lords found that clause 23(g) did not cover the situation, but that withdrawal alone did not constitute a breach by the employer. The risk of delays caused by withdrawal lay with the contractor. However, the employer had a duty to renominate within a reasonable time, and failure to do so could constitute a relevant event under clause 23(g) (failure to issue necessary instructions).

5.54   Where the sub-contractor is named in an instruction relating to a provisional sum, the contractor may make reasonable objection to the named sub-contractor, but must do so within 14 days of the date of issue of the instruction (Schedule 2:5). Otherwise, the contractor must enter into the sub-contract, using documents as described above. The contract does not say what will happen if an objection is made; if the objection is reasonable the contract administrator would have to name another person in a further instruction, or issue instructions to remove the impediment as described above. If a dispute arises this could be referred to adjudication. The instruction naming the sub-contractor is to be valued under the rules in clause 5·2. Delays arising from compliance with the instruction would be grounds for an extension of time under clause 2·20·2·2 and loss/expense under clause 4·18·2·2, and as above, delays in issuing the instructions could give rise to claims under clauses 2·20·6 and 4·18·4, or even to termination.

5.55   Once the sub-contract is entered into, the contractor is entirely responsible for the work carried out by the sub-contractor, and delays on the part of the sub-contractor are not grounds for an extension of time or direct loss and/or expense. Responsibility for payment also rests entirely with the contractor. The contract administrator is therefore not concerned with the details of the sub-contract terms, and the contractor is not required to send a copy of the executed ICSub/NAM/A to either the contract administrator or the employer. If the contract administrator would prefer to have a copy, then the contract should be amended accordingly.

5.56   Under certain circumstances the contract administrator may be obliged to name a replacement sub-contractor. This could occur if the named sub-contractor's employment is terminated by the contractor or the named sub-contractor terminates its own employment (Schedule 2:7). The termination procedures are discussed at paragraphs 9.27 to 9.32 below.

Work not forming part of the contract/persons engaged by the employer

5.57   Under clause 2·7 the employer may engage persons direct to carry out work that does not form part of the contract, while the main contractor is still in possession. This may include statutory undertakers when employed by the employer, but not where they are carrying out the work in pursuance of their statutory duties. If the contract documents have included this requirement, then the contractor must permit the employer to execute such work. Otherwise the employer can only do this with the contractor's consent. The consent may not be unreasonably delayed or withheld.

5.58   Clauses 6·1 and 6·2 make it clear that for the purposes of insurance the contractor is not responsible for the directly engaged person. The employer should therefore ensure that insurance cover is arranged in respect of any act or neglect of the persons to be employed. The employer should also be made fully aware that any disruption caused to the contractor's working could lead to a claim for an extension of time (cl 2·20·6), to loss and expense (cl 4·18·4), or even to the contractor terminating its employment under the contract (cl 8·9·2·2). The employer is therefore at considerable risk, and should be advised to avoid this route if at all possible.

Making good defects

5.59   Following the rectification period the contractor is required to make good any 'defects, shrinkages or other faults … which appear and are notified by the Architect/Contract Administrator to the Contractor' (cl 2·30). The defects are limited to those that result from the works not having been carried out in accordance with the contract. This does not include other defects that may be due, for example, to errors in the design information supplied to the contractor, or to general wear and tear resulting from occupation by the employer, or shrinkages which would be expected even if the works had been carried out as specified. The contractor is similarly not liable for frost damage that occurs after practical completion.

5.60   The obligation does not appear to be limited to those defects that appear after practical completion, and therefore could extend to defects that were patent at that time (note that the wording differs from that in SBC11). It is suggested that the obligation would include defects caused by frost occurring before practical completion.

5.61   However, it is important to note that the obligation to make good appears to be limited to those defects notified by the contract administrator. It is therefore important that the contract administrator prepares a comprehensive schedule. The contract administrator should issue the notification not later than 14 days after the end of the rectification period, the only point where the contract requires the contract administrator to issue such a schedule. The contract administrator may require the contractor to make good a defect at an earlier stage, but this should only be used for serious and urgent problems. No special format is required for the notification, but it is common practice to issue it in the form of an instruction.

5.62   If the contract administrator, with the agreement of the employer, decides to accept any defective work then this should be confirmed by means of an instruction and an amount is deducted from the contract sum (cl 2·30 and 4·8·3). Care should be taken to establish the full extent of the problem before such a course of action is taken, and an appropriate deduction from the contract sum agreed, as it is unlikely that the employer would thereafter be able to claim for consequential problems or further remedial work.

5.63   Once satisfied that all the notified defects have been made good, the contract administrator must issue a certificate to that effect (cl 2·31). The certificate is one of the preconditions to the issue of the final certificate. Note that a separate certificate will be needed for the 'Relevant Part' if the partial possession provisions have been brought into operation (cl 2·27), and that separate certificates will be needed for each section if the sectional completion provisions have been used.

5.64   The contract does not state what should happen in respect of defects that appear after the issue of the certificate but before the issue of the final certificate. It is, however, clear from clause 2·30 that the contract administrator no longer has the power to instruct that these are made good. It is suggested that in such circumstances there would be two possible courses of action. The first would be to make an agreement with the contractor to rectify the defects before the final certificate is issued. If the contractor refused to do this, an amount could be deducted from the contract sum to cover the cost of making good the work, but this would involve some risk to the employer. The second and less risky course would be to have the defective work rectified by another contractor, and deduct the amount paid from the contract sum. This would involve a delay in the issue of the final certificate and would probably be disputed by the contractor.

5.65   The contractor's liability for defective work does not end with the final certificate, except to the limited extent in which the final certificate is conclusive. The contractor is still liable for losses suffered, but no longer has the right to return to site to correct defective work. The employer's remedy is to bring an action at common law. The rectification period therefore is a sensible procedure that benefits the parties in affording an opportunity to remedy problems at a reasonable cost, without the problems associated with bringing a legal action. Nevertheless, if the contract administrator fails to notify the contractor of patent defects, although the contractor would still be liable for any defects, if particular difficulty is experienced in getting these remedied at a later date, then the employer may look to the contract administrator for compensation for any losses.

6   Sums properly due

6.1   The contract sum, which will be the tender figure accepted or agreed following negotiation, is entered in Article 2. However, the wording of the contract recognises that, in practice, this is rarely the amount actually paid, and refers in Article 2 to the contract sum 'or such other sum as shall become payable'. It should be noted that the contract sum itself does not change, the provisions refer to adding or subtracting amounts to or from the contract sum to reach an adjusted figure.

6.2   There are many reasons why the amount finally payable will differ from the contract sum. Under IC11 the sum may contain provisional sums or approximate quantities to cover the cost of work that cannot be accurately described or measured until work is underway. If variations to the works are instructed, then the amount payable must be adjusted accordingly. There is also the possibility of claims from the contractor for loss and expense arising from intervening events which could not be foreseen at the time of tendering. Fees or charges in respect of statutory matters which are not allowed for in the contract documents will require an adjustment to the sum. IC11, like most contracts, contains 'fluctuations' provisions allowing for adjustments in the event of changes in statutory charges. If Supplemental Provision 3 is included, the contractor may propose savings that result in an agreed adjustment. VAT is, of course, not included in the contract sum.

6.3   There will therefore almost inevitably be adjustments during the course of the contract, and the required adjustments are summarised in clause 4·2. The clause makes it clear that the only alterations that may be made are those provided for in the terms of the contract. Usually, the ascertained amounts will be added or deducted as appropriate at the periods for certification. Arithmetical errors by the contractor in pricing are not allowed as a cause for adjustment. Errors in the preparation of the contract bills, if used, must be corrected and will then be treated as if they are a variation (cl 2·12·2). Any divergence between the contract drawings and other documents which necessitates an instruction by the contract administrator may also result in a variation (cl 2·13).

An approximate quantity

6.4   Where bills of quantities are used and work can be described in accordance with the Standard Method of Measurement 7th Edition (SMM7), but the quantity involved is uncertain, an 'Approximate Quantity' can be included. The contract administrator is not required to issue any further instruction for the contractor to carry out this work. After it has been carried out, the work is valued under clause 5·2·4.

6.5   Difficulties can arise if the approximate quantity is not a reasonably accurate forecast of the quantity of work required. The valuation must then include a fair allowance for the difference in quantity over and above the rates or prices tendered by the contractor (cl 5·3·1·4 and 5·3·1·5). The inaccuracy is also an event which may give rise to an extension of time under clause 2·20·4 and a 'Relevant Matter' for direct loss or expense under clause 4·18·3.

Provisional sums

6.6   Where bills of quantities are used but it is not possible to provide sufficient information at the time of tender to allow an item to be described and measured according to the SMM7 rules, then a provisional sum may be inserted in the bills to cover the item. The contract administrator must issue instructions with regard to the expenditure of any provisional sums (cl 3·13) and the contractor can take no action until receiving an instruction. The work is then valued under the valuation rules described below for a variation (cl 5·2·3) and the effect of the instruction will depend on whether the provisional sum is for defined work or for undefined work.

Defined work

6.7   Under clause 1·1 the contract makes reference to a provisional sum being for defined or undefined work as described in Rule 10 of SMM7. The information required to place provisional work in the defined category is the construction of the work, how and where the work fits into the building, the scope and extent of the work and any specific limitations on method or sequence or timing. In other words, the description must be sufficiently detailed for the contractor to make proper allowance for the effect of the work when pricing the relevant preliminaries, and to allow for the work in the programme.

6.8   If the information provided is not as detailed as the rule requires, or if it is erroneous, then a corrective instruction is required from the contract administrator. This is to be treated as a variation (cl 5·5·3), and could give rise to a notice of delay and an application for reimbursement of direct loss and expense from the contractor.

Undefined work

6.9   A provisional sum for undefined work will be applicable where it is not possible to supply the amount of information needed to comply with Rule 10.3 of SMM7. The contractor will not have been able to make proper allowance for the work in programming, planning or the pricing of preliminaries. A provisional sum in this category should not only be sufficient to cover the net cost, but should also take into account the fact that there might be additions to preliminaries, attendance, etc. as an allowance must be made when valuing the instruction. There is also a risk that the contractor might give notice of delay arising from the contract administrator's instruction. Unlike an instruction for the expenditure of a provisional sum for defined work, that for a provisional sum for undefined work could be a relevant event (cl 2·20·2·1) and a relevant matter for which a loss and expense application can be made (cl 4·18·2·1).

6.10   Provisional sums may be included for items that are not specifically work, for example testing, site boards, site facilities, etc. The heading in the bills of quantities will simply be 'include the Provisional Sum of … for', or some other appropriate wording. For work to be carried out by statutory authorities it is suggested that the description of the work be followed by a similar heading.

Valuation of variations

6.11   The contract states that the value of variations is either as agreed between the contractor and employer, or as assessed by the quantity surveyor (cl 5·2). Agreement on a saving could be reached using optional Supplemental Provision 3. Otherwise, the contract does not set out any procedure for reaching an agreement, but in practice it would be open to the contract administrator to request a statement from the contractor, and then, if it is acceptable, to accept the price on behalf of the employer, provided the employer has been consulted and has agreed to the figure. It is generally preferable to agree the value of variations as the project progresses, ideally before the work is carried out, but in some cases, perhaps because the contractor is unable to provide a statement, or because time is short, it will not be possible to reach such an agreement.

6.12   If the quantity surveyor is to value variations, the valuation must be conducted according to the valuation rules set out in clauses 5·3 to 5·6 (Figure 13). Clause 5·3·1 includes for:

- work of similar character undertaken under similar conditions and where the quantity does not change significantly (cl 5·3·1·1);

- work of similar character but not undertaken under similar conditions and/or where the quantity changes significantly (cl 5·3·1·2);

- work not of similar character (cl 5·3·1·3).

Figure 13 Valuation rules

Type of work	Characteristics	Valuation	
Additional or substituted work	5·3·1·1 • Similar character • Similar conditions • Not significant change of quantity	Priced document	5·3·3 • Measurement in accordance with contract bills • Allowance in percentage or lump sum adjustments • Allowance for preliminary items
	5·3·1·2 • Similar character • Not similar conditions • Significant change of quantity	Priced document as basis. Allowance for difference in conditions and quantity	
	5·3·1·3 • Not similar character	Fair rates and prices	
Approximate quantity	5·3·1·4 • Reasonably accurate forecast	Rate or price for that approximate quantity	
	5·3·1·5 • Not reasonably accurate forecast	As above, but with an additional allowance for the difference in quantity	
Omission	5·3·2 Omission of work	Priced document as basis	

6.13   In the first two cases, bills of quantities' rates and prices are to be used in assessing the value of the variation, and it should be noted that the work is not necessarily identical, and that the contractual rates must be used even where those figures contain errors (*Henry Boot Construction Ltd* v *Alstom Combined Cycles*). In the third case, the work should be valued at 'fair rates and prices'. Dissimilar conditions might include, for example, that the instructed work is carried out in winter, whereas under the bills it had been assumed it would be carried out in summer. Such an assumption, however, would have to be clear from an objective analysis of the contract documents (*Wates Construction* v *Bredero Fleet*).

Henry Boot Construction Ltd v *Alstom Combined Cycles* [2000] BLR 247

By a contract formed in 1994, Alstom Combined Cycles employed Henry Boot to carry out civil engineering works in connection with a combined cycle gas turbine power station for PowerGen plc at Connah's Quay in Clwyd. During post-tender negotiations, a price of £258,850 was agreed for temporary sheet piling to trench excavations. Disputes arose regarding the valuation of this work, and these disputes were initially taken to arbitration. The arbitrator found that the agreed figure contained errors that effectively benefited Boot. Boot argued that, nevertheless, the figure should be used to value the work under clause 52(1). The arbitrator decided that clause 52(1) (a) and (b) were inapplicable, and that 52(2) should be applied to achieve a fair valuation. Boot appealed to the Technology and Construction Court, and Judge Humphrey Lloyd decided that the mistake made no difference; the agreed rate should be used even if the results were unreasonable. Clause 52(2) created only a limited exception where the scale or nature of the variation itself made it unreasonable to use the contract rates.

Wates Construction (South) Ltd v *Bredero Fleet Ltd* (1993) 63 BLR 128

Wates Construction entered into a contract on JCT80 to build a shopping centre for Bredero. Some sub-structural work differed from that shown on the drawings and disputes arose regarding the valuation of the works, which were taken to arbitration. In establishing the conditions under which, according to the contract, it had been assumed that the work would be carried out, the arbitrator took into account pre-tender negotiations and the actual knowledge that Wates gained as a result of the negotiations, including proposals that had been put forward at that time. Wates appealed and the court found that the arbitrator had erred by taking this extrinsic information into consideration. The conditions under which the works were to be executed had to be derived from the express provisions of the bills, drawings and other contract documents.

6.14   Work for which an approximate quantity is included in the contract documents is valued at the stated rates and prices under clause 5·3·1·4, except that where the approximate quantity was not a reasonably accurate forecast of the amount of work carried out, the stated rates and prices shall be the basis for valuation and a fair allowance for the difference is to be included (cl 5·3·1·5).

6.15   Work not of similar character should be valued at 'fair rates and prices' (cl 5·3·1·3). Where the appropriate basis of a fair valuation is daywork (when the additional or substituted work cannot be properly valued by measurement) clause 5·4 sets out the rules to be followed in assessing the amount. Otherwise it would be the responsibility of the quantity surveyor in the first instance to determine what a fair rate might be. If the contractor disagrees with this assessment, and the dispute cannot be resolved amicably, then the contractor could take the matter to arbitration.

Reimbursement of direct loss and/or expense

6.16   The objective of clause 4·17 is to enable the contractor to be reimbursed for direct loss and/or direct expense suffered as a result of deferment of possession or disruption to progress, and for which the contractor is not reimbursed under any other provision in the contract. As an alternative, the contractor may be able to pursue this as a claim for general damages for breach of contract at common law, but this would need to be done through adjudication, arbitration or litigation.

6.17   The contractor must apply in writing, otherwise the contract administrator has no power or obligation to deal with loss and expense. The application must be submitted promptly, in fact the use of the phrase 'is likely to incur' suggests an anticipatory quality. No particular format is specified but the application should be supported by such detail as is reasonably necessary, including identifying all 'matters' concerned (*London Borough of Merton* v *Leach*). The contract administrator or quantity surveyor can request additional information.

London Borough of Merton v *Stanley Hugh Leach Ltd* (1985) 32 BLR 51 (ChD)

Stanley Hugh Leach entered into a contract on JCT63 with the London Borough of Merton to construct 287 dwellings. The contract was substantially delayed and a dispute arose regarding this delay and related claims for loss and expense. The dispute went to arbitration and the arbitrator made an interim award on a number of matters. Merton appealed and the court considered 15 questions framed as preliminary issues. Among other things, the court stated that applications for direct loss and/or expense must be made in sufficient detail to enable the architect to form an opinion as to whether there is any loss and/or expense to be ascertained. If there is, then it is the responsibility of the architect to obtain enough information to reach a decision. This responsibility could, of course, include requests for information from the contractor. The court also held that the application must be made within a reasonable time and not so late that the architect was no longer able to form an opinion on matters relevant to the application.

6.18   Claims under clause 4.17 can only be made for loss and expense suffered through deferment of possession, or the particular relevant matters listed in clause 4·18. Other losses are irrecoverable under the contract, although disputed claims may be referred to adjudication, arbitration or litigation. (Note that costs due to suspension under clause 4·13·1 are now handled separately, see paragraph 7.23.) The matters listed in clause 4·18 are concerned with situations where the loss or expense is attributable to the employer, including 'any impediment, prevention or default, whether by act or omission, by the Employer', but excluding the neutral causes which feature in the extension of time provisions of clause 2·20. Some losses caused by the contractor are specifically excluded by the contract; for example, the contractor is not entitled to any adjustment for losses due to failure to supply design information, including failure to comply with a written request from the contract administrator specifying a date by which it is reasonably necessary to receive relevant information (cl 2·14·2).

6.19   Clause 4·17 refers to regular progress of the works being 'materially affected' by the relevant matter. This could include situations where an overall delay to the programme is experienced (often termed 'prolongation') for which an extension of time may have been awarded. However, it can also include disruption to the planned sequence which does not cause any overall delay, provided it can be shown that losses were suffered as a result. Any disruption claim should be related to the progress necessary to complete the works by the completion date, not necessarily the actual sequences of events on site.

6.20   The sums that can be awarded can include any loss or expense that has arisen directly as the result of the relevant matter. The loss and expense award is, in effect, an award of damages and the contract administrator should approach its assessment on the same principles as a court would when awarding damages for breach of contract. In broad terms, the object of the award is to put the contractor back into the position in which it would have been but for the disturbance. The contractor ought to be able to show that it has taken reasonable steps to mitigate its loss, and the losses must have been reasonably foreseeable as likely to result from the 'matter' at the time the contract was entered into. The following are items which could be included: increased preliminaries; overheads; loss of profit; uneconomic working; increases due to inflation; and interest or finance charges.

6.21   The items claimed must be things which the contractor could not recover under any other term of the contract (e.g. it must not duplicate a claim under clause 5·2). Prolongation costs, such as on-site overheads, would normally only be claimable for periods following the date for completion. (For head office overheads, etc., see *McAlpine* v *Property and Land Contractors*.) Interest may also be recoverable, but only if it can be proved to have been a genuine loss (*F G Minter* v *WHTSO*). As clause 4·17 refers to losses which the contractor is 'likely to incur', the award need not be restricted to losses suffered prior to the time when the contractor's application is made, but could include those suffered up until the date of the ascertainment (this would apply particularly to financing charges), and could arguably be extended to losses that could be predicted as likely to occur up until the date the reimbursement is made.

Alfred McAlpine Homes North Ltd v *Property and Land Contractors Ltd* (1995) 76 BLR 59

An appeal arose on a question of law arising out of an arbitrator's award regarding the basis for awarding direct loss and expense with respect to additional overheads and hire of small plant, following an instruction to postpone the works. The judgment contains useful guidance on the basis for awarding direct loss and expense. To 'ascertain' means to 'find out for certain'. It is not necessary to differentiate between 'loss' or 'expense' in a head of claim. Regarding overheads, a contractor would normally be entitled to recover as a 'loss' the shortfall in the contribution that the volume of work had been expected to make to the fixed head office overheads, but which, because of a reduction in volume and revenue caused by the prolongation, was not in fact realised. The fact that the 'Emden' or 'Hudson' formulae depend on certain assumptions means that they are frequently inappropriate. The losses on the plant should be the true cost to the contractor, not based on notional or assumed hire charges.

F G Minter Ltd v *Welsh Health Technical Services Organisation* (1980) 13 BLR 1 (CA)

Minter was employed by Welsh Health Technical Services Organisation (WHTSO) under JCT63 to construct the University Hospital of Wales (second phase) Teaching Hospital. During the course of the contract, several variations were made, and the progress of the works was impeded by the lack of necessary drawings and information. The contractor was paid amounts in respect of direct loss and/or expense, but the amounts paid were challenged as insufficient. The amounts had not been certified and paid until long after the losses had been incurred, therefore the figures should have included an allowance in respect of finance charges or interest. Following arbitration, several questions were put to the High Court, including whether Minter was entitled to finance charges in respect of any of the following periods:

(a)   between the loss and/or expense being incurred and the making of a written application for the same;

(b)   during the ascertainment of the amount; and/or

(c)   between the time of such ascertainment and the issue of the certificate including the ascertained amount.

The court answered 'no' to all three questions and Minter appealed. The Court of Appeal ruled that the answer was 'yes' to the first question and 'no' to the others.

6.22   The contractor must provide full details and particulars of all items concerned with the alleged loss or expense. These should identify which of the losses claimed relate to each of the relevant matters that have occurred. This is sometimes compromised by the use of a 'rolled up' or composite claim approach, where it is not really practicable to separate and itemise the effect of a number of causes. This approach has been accepted by the courts, provided that as much detail as possible has been given, and provided that all disturbance was due to matters under clause 4·18, and not caused by the contractor.

6.23   Formulae such as the 'Hudson' or 'Emden' formulae are sometimes used for estimating head office overheads and profit, which may be difficult to substantiate. These formulae can only be used when it has been established that there has been a loss of this nature. To do this the contractor must be able to show that, but for the delay, the contractor would have been able to earn the amounts claimed on another contract, e.g. by producing evidence such as invitations to tender which were declined. Such formulae may be useful where it is difficult to quantify the amount of the alleged loss, provided a check is made that the assumptions on which the formula is based apply.

6.24   Although direct loss and/or expense are matters of money, not time, which are quite separate issues, there is often a practical correlation in the case of prolongation. Any general implication, however, that there is a link would be incorrect and, in principle, disruption claims and delay to progress are independent. An extension of time, for example, is not a condition precedent to the award of direct loss and/or expense (*H Fairweather & Co.* v *Wandsworth*, see paragraph 4.27).

6.25   Though the contract administrator may delegate the duty of ascertaining the direct loss and expense, it does not appear that it is obligatory to accept the quantity surveyor's opinion (*R Burden* v *Swansea Corporation*), although the quantity surveyor's assessment would be strong evidence as to what the correct amount should be. Applications or claims from the contractor made under the contract must be dealt with according to the procedures of the contract. Failure to certify an amount properly due will not prevent recovery, and may leave the employer liable in damages for breach of contract (*Croudace Ltd* v *London Borough of Lambeth*).

R Burden Ltd v *Swansea Corporation* [1957] 3 All ER 243 (HL)

Burden entered into a contract with Swansea Corporation to build a school. The contract provided for interim certificates to be issued at intervals by the architect. The architect, who was the Corporation's Borough Architect, acted originally as both architect and surveyor under the contract. Later, after 20 certificates had been issued, the firm of quantity surveyors which had originally prepared the bills was appointed to act as surveyor under the contract in place of the Borough Architect. In the next certificate the surveyor reduced the amount applied for by the contractor by around 75 per cent, and the architect certified the lower figure. The surveyor later discovered that it had made a mistake, but did not inform the architect of the error. The contractor gave notice determining the contract, on the grounds that the employer had interfered with the issue of the certificate. The House of Lords decided that a mistake in a direction as to the amount to be paid did not amount to interference or obstruction. It was suggested that the architect would have been at liberty to have certified a different amount if aware of the error.

Croudace Ltd v *London Borough of Lambeth* (1986) 33 BLR 20 (CA)

Croudace entered into an agreement with the London Borough of Lambeth to erect 148 dwelling houses, some shops and a hall. The contract was on JCT63 and the architect was Lambeth's Chief Architect and the quantity surveyor was its Chief Quantity Surveyor. The architect delegated his duties to a private firm of architects. Croudace alleged that there had been delays and that they had suffered direct loss and/or expense and sent letters detailing the matters to the architects. In reply, the architects told Croudace that they had been instructed by Lambeth that all payments relating to 'loss and expense' had to be approved by the Borough. The Chief Architect then retired and was not immediately replaced. There were considerable delays pending the appointment of a successor and Croudace began legal proceedings. The High Court found that Lambeth was in breach of contract in failing to take the necessary steps to ensure that the claim was dealt with, and was liable to Croudace for this breach. The Court of Appeal upheld this finding.

Fluctuations

6.26   In some projects it may be an advantage to insist on a 'fixed' or 'guaranteed' price, whereby the contractor accepts the risk of all changes in the cost of the works due to statutory revisions and market price fluctuations. However, requiring this degree of certainty will, in some economic climates, result in higher tender figures as the contractor will need to allow for possible increases, particularly if the contract period is relatively lengthy. In order to avoid inflated tenders, most contracts allow for some 'fluctuations', whereby the employer accepts some of these risks.

6.27   In IC11 the fluctuations provisions are covered in clauses 4·15 and 4·16, which refer to Schedule 4. Clause 4·15 covers contributions, levy and tax changes, and clause 4·16 covers fluctuations to the contract sum in respect of the work of named sub-contractors.

6.28   Schedule 4 provides for full recovery of all fluctuations in the rates of contributions, levies and taxes in the employment of labour, and in the rates of duties and taxes on the procurement of materials. In short, the only amounts payable are those arising out of an Act of Parliament or delegated legislation. Contractors, however, have pointed out that many less obvious increases are nevertheless not included, therefore a 'percentage addition' is made to allow for these. The agreed percentage is entered in the contract particulars.

6.29   Where a contract includes for fluctuations, in the absence of anything to the contrary, they will be payable for the whole time the contractor is on site, even though it fails to complete within the contract period (*Peak Construction* v *McKinney Foundations*). There is a so-called 'freezing' provision in IC11 (Schedule 4:9·1) but this depends on the clause 2·19 and 2·20 text being left unamended, and all notices of delay properly dealt with by the contract administrator.

Peak Construction (Liverpool) Ltd v *McKinney Foundations Ltd* (1970) 1 BLR 111 (CA)

Peak Construction Ltd was main contractor on a contract to construct a multi-storey block of flats for Liverpool Corporation. As a result of defective work by nominated sub-contractor McKinney Foundations, work on the main contract was halted for 58 weeks, and the main contractor brought a claim against the sub-contractor for damages. The Official Referee, at first instance, found that the entire 58 weeks was delay caused by the nominated sub-contractor, and awarded £40,000 damages, £10,000 of which was for rises in wage rates during the period. McKinney appealed, and the Court of Appeal found that the award of £10,000 could not be upheld as clause 27 of the main contract entitled Peak Construction to claim this from Liverpool Corporation right up until the time when the work was halted.

6.30   The fluctuations to be added to the contract sum in respect of named sub-contractors are the amounts resulting from the application of the fluctuations provisions in clause 4·15 of ICSub/NAM/C. These are also frozen once the sub-contractor is in a period of culpable delay. In addition, should the period in which the sub-contractor is to complete its work be extended on account of a default of the main contractor, the net amount of fluctuations resulting from the period of extension, although added to the monies due to the sub-contractor, is not added to the contract sum. In other words, although the main contractor must pay to the sub-contractor fluctuations for a period of delay which it has caused the sub-contractor, this amount is not reimbursed by the employer.

7 Certification

7.1   One of the most important duties of the contract administrator under IC11 is the issuing of certificates of payment. Failure to carry out this duty with a reasonable degree of care will put the employer at considerable risk. It is not unheard of for contractors to become insolvent during the course of a contract, and if the certificates have been overvalued the employer may suffer losses which could have been avoided.

7.2   On the other hand, the contractor has a right to be paid what the terms of the contract state is due, and the provisions introduced through the Housing Grants, Construction and Regeneration Act (HGCRA) 1996 were partly as a result of the common occurrence of employers withholding payment without due cause. The contract administrator must therefore administer the provisions fairly, and must not be influenced by any attempt on the part of the employer to delay certification or reduce the amounts shown to suit its own economic circumstances.

7.3   It is quite clear from the well-known case of *Sutcliffe* v *Thackrah* that failure to certify correctly could amount to a breach of duty to the employer. The position is less clear with respect to the contract administrator's duty of care to the contractor. A certifier was found liable to a contractor in the case of *Michael Salliss & Co.* v *Calil and W F Newman & Associates*. Although this appeared to be overtaken in *Pacific Associates Inc.* v *Baxter* (1988) 44 BLR 33 (CA), the latter involved non-standard clauses which, if they had not been present, may have had a significant effect on the outcome.

Sutcliffe v *Thackrah* (1974) 4 BLR 16 (CA)

An architect issued certificates on a contract for the construction of a dwellinghouse. The contractor's employment was determined for proper reasons, following which the contractor was declared bankrupt. It then became apparent that much of the work, which had been included in the interim certificates, was defective, and the architect was found negligent. In the House of Lords, when reviewing the role of the architect, Lord Reid stated (at page 21):

> Many matters may arise in the course of the execution of a building contract where a decision has to be made which will affect the amount of money which the contractor gets. The building owner and the contractor make their contract on the understanding that in all such matters the architect will act in a fair and unbiased manner and it must therefore be implicit in the owner's contract with the architect that he shall not only exercise due care and skill but also reach such decisions fairly, holding the balance between his client and the contractor.

7.4   The payment provisions in IC11 comply with the HGCRA 1996 Part II, as amended by the LDEDCA 2009. The result is a rather complex set of payment provisions, perhaps in some respects out of proportion with what had previously been a relatively simple form.

Nevertheless, the provisions of the 1996 Act are, of course, compulsory for all contracts to which the Act applies, and the remaining clauses should not be amended without taking expert advice. In summary, interim payments are to be made by the employer to the contractor after the issue of certificates by the contract administrator (cl 4·7·2). The contractor may submit its view as to what the certificate should cover by an interim application, but the valuation is a matter for the contract administrator. If no certificate is issued, and an application was made, then the amount stated in the application will become the amount due. Alternatively, if no certificate is issued, and no application was made, after the date for issue of the certificate has passed, the contractor may issue a payment notice. The amount shown in that notice will become the amount payable.

Interim certificates

7.5   The timing of the issue of certificates has changed since IC05. The contract particulars now establish 'due dates' (the first of which is entered in the contract particulars, with subsequent due dates at monthly intervals) and interim certificates are now required to be issued within five days of the due date, and payment made within 14 days of the due date (cl 4·7·1 and 4·11·1). The effect of this clause is that, unless the certificate is actually issued on the due date, the employer will have a shorter period within which it must pay than was the case with IC05. Other time periods, discussed below, are also related to the due date, rather than the date of issue of the certificate. Certificates are issued to the employer and a duplicate sent to the contractor (cl 1·8).

7.6   There is also an optional provision for advance payment to the main contractor, provided the employer is not a local authority (cl 4·6). An entry must be made in the contract particulars to show whether or not the optional provision is to apply. If it is, the amount will be entered as either a fixed sum or a percentage of the contract sum. The entry must also show when it is to be paid to the contractor, and when it is to be reimbursed to the employer. A bond may be required, and IC11 includes an advance payment bond as Part 1 of Schedule 3: Forms of Bonds.

7.7   There is always a risk in making an advance payment with respect to a construction contract, even when backed by a bond, and the procedure will inevitably involve extra expense to the employer. The employer should be quite clear as to what compensatory benefits, such as a reduction in the contract sum, will result before agreeing to any arrangement of this sort. In the end it is the employer's decision, but the contract administrator may need to explain the provisions and give initial advice.

Valuations and ascertainment of amounts due

7.8   There are two methods by which the amount due to the contractor as interim payments can be assessed: either through acceptance of the figure stated in a contractor's application for payment, or through valuation by the quantity surveyor. The latter has traditionally been the basis for assessing payments under JCT forms.

7.9   Clause 4·10 gives the contractor the right to submit its own assessment (an 'Interim Application') of the value of an interim certificate. The application must be made at least seven days before the due date and should be sent direct to the quantity surveyor. It is then open to the quantity surveyor to agree or disagree with this valuation. However IC11, unlike IC05, does not require the quantity surveyor to identify in detail the matters where any differences arise and inform the contractor. The contract administrator should request that the quantity surveyor forwards copies of all correspondence and keeps the contract administrator informed regarding applications.

7.10   Whether or not an interim application is received, the quantity surveyor will normally carry out a valuation prior to the due date (a valuation is necessary to determine whether the contractor's application is correct). The valuation should cover the amounts due at a date not more than seven days before the issue of the certificate. Valuations by the quantity surveyor can be made 'whenever the Architect/Contract Administrator considers them necessary' (cl 4·7·3). The roles of the quantity surveyor and the contract administrator, however, are quite distinct, and it is ultimately for the contract administrator to decide the figure to be shown on the certificate.

Coverage of the certificate

7.11   Clause 4·7·2 requires that interim certificates state not only the amount to be paid, but also 'the basis on which that sum has been calculated'. It is unlikely that a great deal of detail will be required here; a short schedule will probably be sufficient. Similar provisions are included for the final certificate.

7.12   The amount certified is the total amount ascertained under clauses 4·8·1 and 4·8·2, less any ascertained amounts of any deductions as set out in clause 4·8·3. The amounts to be included can be summarised as follows:

- 95 per cent (or other proportion stated in the contract particulars) of the following (cl 4·8·1):

    - total value of work properly executed (cl 4·8·1·1);
    - total value of materials and goods properly on site (cl 4·8·1·2);
    - value of off-site materials, goods or items, provided they are 'Listed Items' (cl 4·8·1·3 and 4·9);

- 100 per cent of the following items, if applicable (cl 4·8·2):

    - fees and charges (cl 2·3);
    - inspections and tests (cl 3·14 and 3·15·3);
    - costs and expenses (cl 4.13)
    - fluctuations (cl 4·15 and 4·16);
    - loss and expense (cl 4·17);
    - insurance monies (cl 2·6, 6·5, 6·10, 6·11 and Schedule 1);
    - sums for restoration of damaged work (Schedule 1).

Value of work properly executed

7.13   The contract administrator should only certify after having carried out an inspection to a reasonably diligent standard. Contract administrators should not include any work that appears not to have been properly executed, whether or not it is about to be remedied or the retention is adequate to cover remedial work (*Townsend* v *Stone Toms* and *Sutcliffe* v *Chippendale & Edmondson*). Contract administrators should also note the recent case of *Dhamija* v *Sunningdale Joineries Ltd*, which stated that a quantity surveyor is not responsible for determining the quality of work executed. Where work which has been included in a certificate subsequently proves to be defective, the value can be omitted from the next certificate. It is arguable, however, whether the contract administrator has the power to issue a 'negative' certificate, i.e. a repayment by the contractor. Unlike the final payment provisions (cl 4·14·2), clause 4·11 does not expressly refer to repayments. In addition, clause 4·12·2 states that 'the amount may be zero' but does not refer to negative amounts. This clause derives from the LDEDCA 2009, and on balance it seems unlikely that the contract will be interpreted to allow for negative payments. If such a situation arises, it may be sensible to seek legal advice, particularly if the amount is significant.

Townsend v *Stone Toms & Partners* (1984) 27 BLR 26 (CA)

Mr Townsend engaged Stone Toms as architect in connection with the renovation of a farmhouse in Somerset. John Laing Construction Ltd was employed to carry out the work on JCT67 Fixed Fee Form of Prime Cost Contract. Following the end of the defects liability period, the architect issued an interim certificate that included the value of work which had already been included in the schedule of defects, and which the architect knew had not yet been put right. Mr Townsend brought proceedings against both Stone Toms and Laing. Laing made a payment into court of £30,000, which was accepted by Mr Townsend in full and final settlement. Mr Townsend then continued with the proceedings against the architect, claiming that he was entitled to recover any excess that he might have obtained from Laing had he continued with those proceedings. The Official Referee assessed the total value of the claims against Laing as only £25,000, therefore no excess was recoverable. The Deputy Official Referee also found that the architect was not negligent in issuing the interim certificate. Mr Townsend appealed and the Court of Appeal, although approving the lower court's decision on the effect of the payment into court, held that the architect had been negligent. Oliver LJ stated (at page 46):

> the whole purpose of the certification is to protect the client from paying to the builder more than the proper value of the work done, less proper retention, before it is due. If the architect deliberately over-certifies work which he knows has not been done properly, this seems to be a clear breach of his contractual duty, and whether certification is described as 'negligent' or 'deliberate' is immaterial'.

Sutcliffe v *Chippendale & Edmondson* (1971) 18 BLR 149
(Note: this case is the first instance decision which was appealed to the Court of Appeal *sub nom. Sutcliffe* v *Thackrah*, discussed at paragraph 7.3.)

Mr Sutcliffe engaged the architect Chippendale & Edmondson in relation to a project to build a new house. No terms of engagement were agreed, but the architect proceeded to design the house, invite tenders and arrange for the appointment of a contractor on JCT63. Work progressed slowly and towards the end of the work it became obvious that much of the work was defective. The architect had issued ten interim certificates before Mr Sutcliffe entirely lost confidence, dismissed the architect and threw the contractor off the site. He then had the work completed by another contractor and other consultants at a cost of around £7,000, in addition to which he was obliged, as a result of the original contractor having obtained judgment against him, to pay all ten certificates in full. As this contractor was then declared bankrupt, Mr Sutcliffe brought a claim against the architect. The architect contended, among other things, that its duty of supervision did not extend to informing the quantity surveyor of defective work that should be excluded from the valuation. His Honour Judge Stabb QC found for Mr Sutcliffe, stating 'I do not accept that the words "work properly executed" can include work not then properly executed but which it is expected, however confidently, the Contractor will remedy in due course' (at page 166).

Dhamija and another v *Sunningdale Joineries Ltd and others* [2010] EWHC 2396 (TCC)

The claimants brought an action against the building contractor, the architect and the quantity surveyor (McBains) arising out of alleged defects in the design and construction of their home. There had been no written or oral contract with the quantity surveyor, but the claimants argued that there was an implied term that the quantity surveyor would only value work that had been properly executed by the contractor and was not obviously defective. The court held that a quantity surveyor's terms of engagement would include an implied term that the quantity surveyor act with the reasonable skill and care of a quantity surveyor of ordinary competence and experience when valuing the works for the purposes of interim certificates. However, the judge held that the quantity surveyor would not owe an implied duty to exclude the value of defective works from valuations, however obvious the defects. This was the exclusive responsibility of the architect appointed under the contract. Furthermore, the quantity surveyor owed no implied duty to report the existence of defects to the architect.

7.14 The value of the work will be calculated using the rates shown in the priced document, with any work resulting from variations valued as set out under the valuation rules. If a priced activity schedule is included, the amount included in any interim certificate in respect of any items listed in the activity schedule should be the total of the amounts reached by multiplying the percentage of the work properly executed by the price for that work as shown on the activity schedule. The fact that an activity schedule is used, however, does not lessen the contract administrator's duty to determine that all work certified has been carried out in accordance with the contract.

Unfixed materials

7.15 The interim certificate should include materials which have been delivered to the site but are not yet incorporated in the works (cl 4·8·1·2). In spite of detailed provisions aimed at protecting the employer, there remains some risk in including these items. Once materials have been built in, under common law they would normally become the property of the owner of the land, irrespective of whether or not they have been paid for by the contractor. This would be the case even if there were a retention of title clause in the contract with the sub-contractor or supplier. A retention of title clause is one which stipulates that the goods sold do not become the property of the purchaser until they have been paid for, even if they are in the possession of the purchaser.

7.16   The employer could be at risk, however, where materials have not yet been built in, even where the materials have been certified and paid for. The contractor might not actually own the materials paid for because of a retention of title clause in the sale of materials contract. Under the Sale of Goods Act 1979, sections 16 to 19, property in goods normally passes when the purchaser has possession of them, but a retention of title clause will be effective between a supplier and a contractor even where the contractor has been paid for the goods, provided they have not yet been built in. It should be noted, however, that the employer may have some protection through the operation of section 25 of the Act, which in some circumstances allows the employer to treat the contractor as having authority to transfer the title in the goods, even though this may not in fact be the case (see *Archivent* v *Strathclyde Regional Council*).

Archivent Sales & Developments Ltd v *Strathclyde Regional Council* (1984) 27 BLR 98 (Court of Session, Outer House)

Archivent agreed to sell a number of ventilators to a contractor who was building a primary school for Strathclyde Regional Council. The contract of sale included the term 'Until payment of the price in full is received by the company, the property in the goods supplied by the company shall not pass to the customer'. The ventilators were delivered and included in a certificate issued under the main contract (JCT63), which was paid. The contractor went into receivership before paying Archivent, which claimed against the Council for the return of the ventilators or a sum representing their value. The Council claimed that section 25(1) of the Sale of Goods Act 1979 operated to give it unimpeachable title. The judge found for the Council. Even though the clause in the sub-contract successfully retained the title for the sub-contractor, the employer was entitled to the benefit of section 25(1) of the Sale of Goods Act 1979. The contractor was in possession of the ventilators and had ostensible authority to pass the title on to the employer, who had purchased them in good faith.

7.17   Another risk relating to rightful ownership is where the contractor fails to pay a domestic sub-contractor that has purchased materials, and the sub-contractor claims ownership of the unfixed materials. Here the risk may be higher, as a work and materials contract is not governed by the Sale of Goods Act 1979. Therefore there can be no assumption that property would pass on possession.

7.18   IC11 attempts to deal with the issues surrounding ownership in several ways. First, unfixed materials and goods, which have been delivered to the site and are intended for the works, may not be removed without the written consent of the contract administrator (cl 2·17). Removal would be a breach of contract, therefore the employer could claim from the contractor for any losses suffered through unauthorised removal. This would apply even though the materials or goods may not yet have been included in any certificate. Second, unfixed materials and goods, either on or off site, which have been included in a certificate that has been paid, are to become the property of the employer (cl 2·17), and the contractor is thereby prevented from disputing ownership.

7.19   Clause 2·17 of the main contract, however, is only binding between the parties, and does not place obligations on any sub-contractor. The risk facing the employer is that, if the contractor becomes insolvent, a sub-contractor or supplier may still have a rightful claim to ownership of the unfixed goods, even though they have been paid for by the employer (see *Dawber Williamson Roofing v Humberside County Council*). The main contract therefore requires that all sub-contracts include similar clauses to 2·17 regarding non-removal from site, and ownership passing upon payment (cl 3·6·2·1). Sub-contracts must include a clause stating that once materials and goods have been certified and paid for under the main contract they become the property of the employer and that the sub-contractor 'shall not deny' this (cl 3·6·2·1·1, with equivalent provisions included in ICSub/NAM/C at cl 2·11). This would operate even where the main contractor has become insolvent. Even this might not protect the employer in some circumstances, because if the sub-contractor does not have 'good title' it cannot pass it on. Thus, for example, it might not prevent a sub-subcontractor claiming ownership.

Dawber Williamson Roofing Ltd v *Humberside County Council* (1979) 14 BLR 70

The plaintiff entered into a sub-contract with Taylor and Coulbeck Ltd (T&C) to supply and fix roofing slates. The main contractor's contract with the defendant was on JCT63. By clause 1 of its sub-contract (which was on DOM/1) the plaintiff was deemed to have notice of all the provisions of the main contract, but it contained no other provisions as to when property was to pass. The plaintiff delivered 16 tons of roofing slates to the site, which were included in an interim certificate, which was paid by the defendant. T&C then went into liquidation without paying the sub-contractor, which brought a claim for the amount or, alternatively, the return of the slates. The judge allowed the claim, holding that clause 14 of JCT63 could only transfer property where the main contractor had a good title. (The difference between this and the Archivent case cited above is that in this case the sub-contract was a contract for work and materials, to which the Sale of Goods Act 1979 did not apply.)

7.20   Under the IC11 provisions, the contract administrator is obliged to include the unfixed materials in an interim certificate, even though this limited risk to the employer remains, provided that the materials are not prematurely delivered and are properly protected. Contract administrators should pay careful attention to the exact wording of this condition (cl 4·8·1·2).

'Listed Items'

7.21   Interim certificates might include amounts in respect of any 'Listed Items' (cl 4·8·1·3). If this provision is to apply, then the list must be attached to the bills of quantities (or specification/schedules of work) to which the contractor has tendered. The listed items may be 'uniquely identified' or not uniquely identified (i.e. materials or goods or items prefabricated for inclusion in the works). The value of items listed must be included in an interim certificate prior to delivery on site, provided certain preconditions are fulfilled:

•   the listed items are in accordance with the contract (cl 4·9·1);

•   the contractor has provided reasonable proof that the property is vested in it (cl 4·9·2·1);

- the contractor provides proof that the items are insured against specified perils until delivery on site (cl 4·9·2·2);

- the listed items are 'set apart' or clearly marked and identified (cl 4·9·3);

- if the item is not 'uniquely identified', or if required in the contract particulars, the contractor has provided a bond (cl 4·9·4, cl 4·9·5 and Part 2 of Schedule 3).

7.22   The contract administrator has no discretionary power to certify any off-site items, other than those that have been listed. This makes the position for both parties clear, in that only 'listed' off-site materials are to be certified. The contract administrator should therefore be careful not to include any unlisted off-site materials in any certificate, as only listed items are covered by the clause 2·18 safeguards to the employer regarding ownership and responsibility for loss or damage.

Costs and expenses due to suspension

7.23   Clause 4.13.2 states that 'Where the Contractor exercises his right of suspension under clause 4·13·1, he shall be entitled to a reasonable amount in respect of costs and expenses reasonably incurred by him as a result of the exercise of the right'. These amounts are also to be included in interim valuations. The phrase 'costs and expenses' is taken from the LDEDCA 2009, and suggests something more limited than the range of losses that could be claimed under a clause 4·17 loss and/or expense claim, for example that it is limited to 'direct and ascertainable costs'. However, a valid suspension would be due to a breach of contract by the employer, for which the contractor would be able to claim damages at common law, so it may be sensible for contract administrators not to interpret this clause too strictly.

Other items in the gross valuation

7.24   In addition to the value of work properly executed and of materials properly on the site, clause 4·8·2 lists other amounts that must be included in the gross valuation for an interim certificate. For example, payments ascertained as due to the main contractor under clause 4·15 (tax, etc. fluctuations), or under clause 4·17 (direct loss and/or expense) are to be added to the contract sum.

Deductions from the gross valuation

Withheld percentage

7.25   Some of the items that must be included in the gross valuation are subject to a reduction of five per cent (cl 4·8·1). If an alternative to five per cent is required then it should be entered in the contract particulars. Half of the withheld amount is released upon practical completion, and the remaining half with the final certificate. The amount is commonly referred to as 'retention' although IC11 does not use this term. The employer is trustee of the withheld percentage for the contractor (cl 4·12·3), but is not obliged to invest it for the contractor, and would have the benefit of any interest which accrues. The employer has the right to deduct from the retention any sums due from the contractor, including sums due by right of set-off.

7.26   Although IC11 contains no provision requiring the employer to place the withheld percentage in a separate banking account, a series of cases have established that such an obligation would be implied in any contract that requires the employer to hold the money as a trustee (see *Rayack* v *Lampeter*, *Wates Construction* v *Franthom Property* and *Finnegan* v *Ford Sellar Morris*). However, the court will not make an order to place money in a separate account following the insolvency of the employer (see *Mac-Jordan Construction* v *Brookmount Erostin*). The contractor would have no special claim beyond that of an unsecured creditor. To be safe the contractor must insist, while the employer is solvent, that the money is placed in a separate account. This dilemma over retention and the effectiveness of trustee status has raised the question of bonds and guarantee bonds from both employer and contractor, respectively, as an alternative.

Rayack Construction Ltd v *Lampeter Meat Co. Ltd* (1979) 12 BLR 30

Rayack Construction agreed to build two meat-processing plants for Lampeter Meat Company at its factory. The contract was a modified version of JCT63 that required payment of certified amounts within 90 days of the date on the certificate, and allowed for 50 per cent retention to be deducted by the employer. The contract also contained a clause similar to clause 4·12·3, which stated that the employer's interest in the retention was fiduciary as trustee for the contractor, but contained no provision requesting that the retention be held in a separate bank account. The court held, nevertheless, that the employer was under an obligation to place the fund in a separate account. The clause would otherwise be of no practical application as it would not protect the contractor from the consequences of the employer's insolvency.

Wates Construction (London) Ltd v *Franthom Property Ltd* (1991) 53 BLR 23 (CA)

Wates entered into a contract with Franthom on JCT80 to construct a hotel in Kent. Clause 30·5·3 (requiring Franthom to place retention in a separate account) had been deleted, but otherwise the retention clauses were, in all material respects, the same as those in IC11. Although requested to do so by Wates, Franthom refused to place the accrued retention of around £84,000 in a separate account. Wates then commenced legal proceedings. Judge Newey ordered Franthom to place the money in a separate account, and Franthom then appealed. The court dismissed the appeal, stating that 'clear express provisions are needed if a separate bank account is not to be set up'. The fact that the clause had been deleted did not, of itself, indicate what the parties' intentions were; the effect was the same as if the words had never been there at all.

J F Finnegan Ltd v *Ford Sellar Morris Developments Ltd* (1991) 53 BLR 38

Finnegan was the contractor on a JCT81 contract for works at Ashford. After the works reached practical completion, the employer claimed liquidated damages of around £60,000 against a sum admitted as due to the contractor of around £20,000. Under clause 30·4·2·2, the employer was obliged to place retention monies deducted in a separate account if requested to do so by the contractor. Finnegan commenced action to recover the sum due. The employer counterclaimed for the liquidated damages and Finnegan then requested that the retention be placed in a separate account. The employer refused and Finnegan applied for an injunction. The judge granted the injunction, despite the fact that this was long after practical completion. The contract did not require that a request was made each time retention was deducted nor at the time it was deducted.

Mac-Jordan Construction Ltd v *Brookmount Erostin Ltd* (1991) 56 BLR 1

A developer held over £100,000 for the contractor in retention money but was also heavily indebted to the bank (floating loan granted by a charge). The developer went into insolvency and the bank appointed administrative receivers. The contractor then sought a court injunction to establish a separate retention fund but the Court of Appeal refused on grounds that this would give an unsecured creditor (the contractor) preference over any other unsecured creditors of an insolvent debtor. The contractor's right to the retention was stated to be no more than an 'unsatisfied and unsecured contractual right for the payment of money' (Scott LJ at page 15).

Advance payments and bonds

7.27 If the parties have elected to use the advance payment provisions, the payment indicated in the contract particulars is paid to the contractor before the first certificate of payment is due for issue, but only after the contractor has provided the bond required (cl 4·6). Payment is made direct from the employer to the contractor, and the contract administrator should ensure receipt of copies of any correspondence regarding this. Details of when the reimbursements are to take place will also be set out in the contract particulars and could, for example, be in stages throughout the project. The reimbursement is deducted from the gross valuation under the relevant certificate. It should be noted that the amount to be deducted each month should be a cumulative total of the reimbursements, with the final deduction equalling the original advance payment, and that final deduction should appear on all subsequent certificates including the final certificate.

Other deductions

7.28 As noted above, the contract administrator may make certain deductions before reaching the gross valuation. These are listed in clause 4·8·3, and include amounts relating to the acceptance of contractor errors (cl 2·9 and 2·30), costs due to failure to comply with instructions (cl 3·9), some insurance costs (cl 6·10) and fluctuation sums. Some others mentioned in the contract are not listed in clause 4·8·3 (e.g. default in taking out insurance, cl 6·4·3) and, although the contract is not clear, it is suggested these could be dealt with by a deduction or by a pay less notice.

VAT

7.29 The contract sum is exclusive of any VAT (cl 4·4·1), and the employer is obliged to pay the contractor any VAT properly chargeable. If any supply to the employer becomes exempt after the base date, then the employer may need to reimburse the contractor for amounts of input tax which it has paid but is unable to recover (cl 4·4·2). As in IC05, the form does not contain detailed provisions regarding VAT, so if particular arrangements are required, then a separate agreement would need to be drawn up.

Payment procedure

7.30   The final date for payment of each interim certificate is 14 days from its due date (cl 4·11·1). It should be noted that this requirement has changed from earlier versions of the form, where the 14 days ran from the date of the certificate so that, unless the certificate is issued on the due date, the time period before payment is required will be reduced. The payment should reach the contractor by the final date for payment, so allowance should be made for posting.

7.31   If the employer intends to withhold any amount from the sum certified, then the contractor must be given written notice of this no later than five days before the final date for payment, in the form of a 'Pay Less Notice' (cl 4·11·5). The pay less notice should set the sum that the employer considers to be due to the contractor at the date on which the notice is given and 'the basis on which that sum has been calculated' (cl 4·12·1·1). If a pay less notice is issued, the employer must pay the contractor at least the sum set out in that notice by the final date for payment (Figure 14).

Payment when no certificate is issued

7.32   The contract contains a remedy in the event that the date for issue should pass without the interim certificate being provided. If it has not already submitted an interim payment application the contractor can, at any time after the issue date has passed, send an interim payment notice to the employer. The notice should state the sum that the contractor 'considers to be or have been due to him at the relevant due date in accordance with clause 4·8 and the basis on which that sum has been calculated' (cl 4·10·2·2). The sum shown on the notice will become the amount due. In the case where the contractor has already submitted an application for payment, it need take no further action, as the application will be considered an interim payment notice (cl 4·10·2·1). Where an interim payment notice is given, clause 4·11·4 states that 'the final date for payment of the sum specified in it shall for all purposes be regarded as postponed by the same number of days as the number of days after expiry of the 5 day period referred to in clause 4·7·2 that the Interim Payment Notice is given'. This is best understood by way of example: if the payment notice was issued six days after the final date for issue of the certificate (i.e. 11 days in total after the due date), the final date for payment would be 20 days after the due date (i.e. 14 plus 6 days). If the employer disagrees with the amount shown on the payment notice, then it must issue a pay less notice as described above (which, in this example, would be within four days of the notice).

Deductions

7.33   The contract expressly gives the employer the right to make certain deductions from the certified sums due to the contractor. Note that these are distinct from amounts that may be deducted before arriving at the sum to be shown on the certificate. The pay less notice might be used in relation to clause 4·8 deductions, but only if these have not already been accounted for as required under the certificate. In addition, the contract refers to other matters not listed in clause 4·8·3 which may be deducted by the employer by means of a notice, for example liquidated damages (cl 2·32·2) and some insurance premiums (cl 6·4·3 and Schedule 3:A·2), all of which should be covered by a pay less notice.

Figure 14 Interim payment procedure

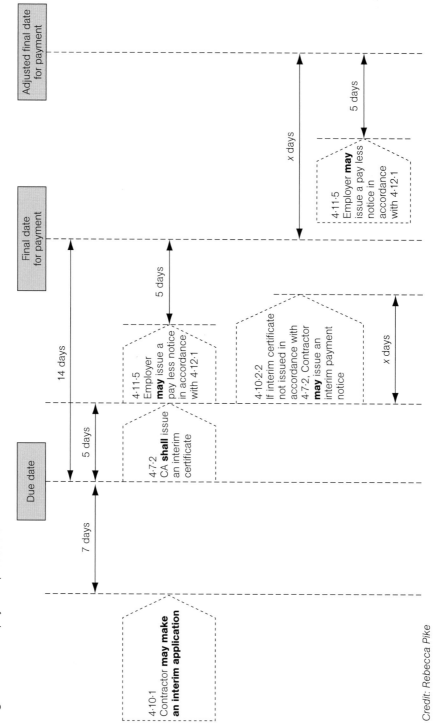

Credit: Rebecca Pike

Employer's obligation to pay

7.34   In addition to the contractual rights to make deductions discussed above, the employer may have other rights to withhold payment under common law. Prior to the HGCRA 1996, it was clear that if the employer had an arguable case that the certificate may have included work which was defective, and therefore had been overvalued, then the employer need not have paid the full amount, but could have raised the losses due to the defects either as a counterclaim in any action brought by the contractor, or as a defence to the claim. The latter process is often termed 'abatement' by lawyers.

7.35   It is now generally agreed that, in cases where such a right may exist, it can only be exercised through the use of the 'Pay Less Notice' procedure as discussed above. The employer would therefore be unable to withhold amounts to cover any defective work included in a certificate, unless the deduction is covered by a notice (*Rupert Morgan Building Services (LLC) Ltd* v *David Jervis and Harriet Jervis*). The rights of the employer when defects appear after the expiry of the time limits for notices, but before the final date for payment, are unclear, but it is arguable that in such situations the employer would retain a right to abatement of the amount due.

Rupert Morgan Building Services (LLC) Ltd v *David Jervis and Harriet Jervis* [2004] BLR 18 (CA)

A couple engaged a builder carry out work on their cottage, by means of a contract on the standard form published by the Architecture and Surveying Institute ('ASI'). The 7th interim certificate was for a sum of around £44,000 plus VAT. The employers accepted that part of that amount was payable but disputed the balance, amounting to approximately £27,000. The builders sought summary judgment for the balance. The employers did not give 'a notice of intention to withhold payment' as required under the contract. The builders argued that it followed, by virtue of HGCRA 1996 section 111(1), that the employers 'may not withhold payment'. The employers maintained that it was open to them by way of defence to prove that the items of work which go to make up the unpaid balance 'were not done at all, or were duplications of items already paid or were charged as extras when they were within the original contract, or represent "snagging" for Works already done and paid for'. The Court of Appeal determined that, in the absence of an effective withholding notice, the employer has no right to set off against a contract administrator's certificate.

Contractor's position if the certificate is not paid

7.36   IC11 includes several provisions which protect the contractor if the employer fails to pay the amounts due to the contractor. Clause 4·11·6 makes provision for simple interest to accrue on any unpaid amount. The defined 'Interest Rate' is set at five per cent over the base rate of the Bank of England, and the interest accrues from the final date for payment until the amount is paid. Similar provisions are included for the final certificate. (It should be noted that if the provision were deleted the contractor would normally have a statutory right to interest under the Late Payment of Commercial Debts (Interest) Act 1998.) If the employer makes a valid deduction following a pay less notice, it is suggested that interest would not be due on this amount. The clause does not refer to the amount stated on the certificate but to 'a sum due to the Contractor under these Conditions', which would take into account valid deductions.

7.37   The contractor is also given a 'right of suspension' under clause 4·13. This right is required by the HGCRA 1996, Part II. If the employer fails to pay the contractor by the final date for payment, the contractor has a right to suspend performance of all its obligations under the contract, which would include not only the carrying out of the work but, for example, could also extend to any insurance obligations. This non-payment is stated to be of 'the sum payable in accordance with clause 4·11', therefore the contractor may not suspend work if a pay less notice has been issued by the employer. The contractor must have given the employer written notice of its intention to suspend work and stated the grounds for the suspension, and the default must have continued for a further seven days. The contractor must resume work when the payment is made. Under these circumstances the suspension would not give the employer the right to terminate the contractor's employment. Any delay caused by the suspension could be a relevant event (cl 2·20·5) and any reasonable costs and expenses incurred are claimable under clause 4·13·3 (see paragraph 7.23).

7.38   The contractor also has the right to terminate its employment if the employer does not pay amounts due (cl 8·9·1·1). The contractor must give notice of this intention, which specifies the default as required by the contract (see paragraph 9.21).

Contractor's position if it disagrees with amount certified

7.39   As a result of the introduction of the interim payment notice provision, it is no longer the case that the issue of a certificate is a condition precedent to the right of the contractor to be paid. However, where a certificate has been issued, the contractor is only entitled to the amount shown, even if it is undervalued and irrespective of what it may have put forward in its interim payment applications (*Lubenham* v *South Pembrokeshire District Council*). This case states that the contractor is only entitled to the sum stated in the certificate, even if the certificate contains an error, for example because it includes a wrongful deduction. The contractor's remedy is to request that the error is corrected in the next certificate, or to bring proceedings (such as adjudication) to have the certificate adjusted. (There are exceptions to this rule where, for example, the employer has interfered with the issue of the certificate, in which case the contractor may be entitled to summary judgment for the correct amount). This appears to be the case even where the interim certificate shows a negative amount, i.e. an amount payable by the contractor to the employer, which may occur if the contract administrator decides that work was overvalued, or there was some other error, in an earlier certificate. Unlike the final certificate, the clauses relating to interim payments do not give the contractor the right to issue a pay less notice.

Lubenham Fidelities and Investments Co. Ltd v *South Pembrokeshire District Council* (1986) 33 BLR 39 (CA)

Lubenham Fidelities was a bondsman which elected to complete two buildings based on JCT63. The architect, Wigley Fox Partnership, issued several interim certificates which stated the total value of work carried out, but also made deductions for liquidated damages and defective work from the face of the certificate. Lubenham protested that the certificates had not been correctly calculated, withdrew its contractors from the site and issued notices to determine the contract. Shortly after the Council gave notice of determination of the contract, Lubenham brought a claim against the Council on the grounds that its notices were valid and effective, and against Wigley Fox on the basis that the architect's negligence had caused it losses. It was held that the Council was not obliged to pay more than the amount on the certificate, and that whatever the cause of the undervaluation the correct procedure was not to withdraw labour, but to request that the error was corrected in the next certificate, or to pursue the matter in arbitration. Lubenham's claim against Wigley Fox failed because it was the suspension of the works rather than the certificates that had caused the losses, and because the architect had not acted with the intention of interfering with the performance of the contract.

Interim payment on practical completion

7.40   An interim certificate is to be issued not later than 14 days after the date of practical completion (cl 4·7·1·2), certifying payment of 97.5 per cent of the value referred to in clause 4·8·1 and the contract particulars and 100 per cent of the value of amounts under clause 4·8·2, together with other deductions as discussed above (see Figure 15). The effect of this certificate is to release to the contractor half of the withheld amounts (retention). The employer retains the right to deduct half the percentage from the outstanding amounts due under this certificate.

7.41   Following practical completion, further payment certificates are issued at two-monthly intervals (cl 4·7·1·3). Although no further work should be carried out during this period (save for instructed remedial work) amounts may nevertheless become due, for example, when a claim for loss and/or expense has not been resolved prior to practical completion. A further interim certificate is also issued at the end of the rectification period or, if later, the date of the certificate of making good (cl 4·7·1·4). The amount of retention deducted from all interim certificates following practical completion is 2.5 per cent or as stated in the contract particulars (cl 4·8·1).

Final certificate

7.42   To summarise, by final certificate stage the following certificates should have been issued:

- interim certificates at monthly intervals (cl 4·7·1·1);

- practical completion certificate (cl 2·21);

- interim certificate following practical completion, including release of half of the retention (cl 4·7·1·2);

- certificates at two-monthly intervals during the rectification period (cl 4·7·1·3);

- certificate of making good (cl 2·31).

7.43   The final certificate must be issued within the specific time periods set out in the contract (see Figure 15). In practice, the latest date for issue tends to be determined by the process of calculating the adjusted contract sum. The onus is on the contractor to send all necessary information to the contract administrator or the quantity surveyor not later

Figure 15 Final payment procedure

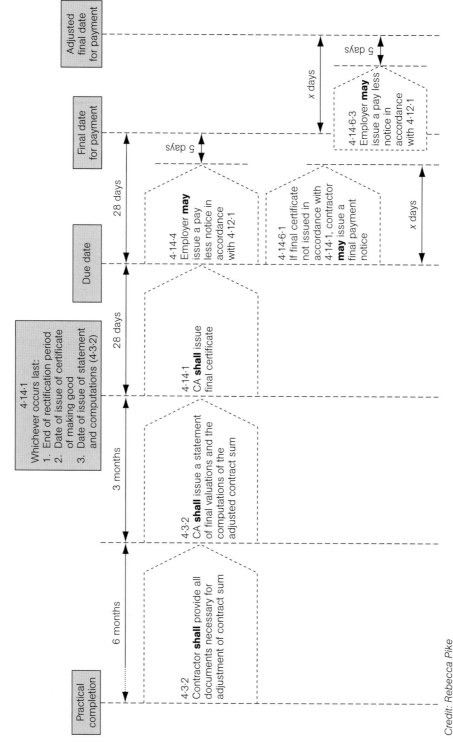

Credit: Rebecca Pike

than six months after practical completion of the works (cl 4·3·2). No later than three months after receiving this information, the contract administrator, or the quantity surveyor if asked to do so, makes a final assessment of the amount due, including any amount of loss and expense, and the quantity surveyor prepares a statement of final adjustment of the contract sum (cl 4·3·2) which must be sent to the contractor within that three-month period.

7.44   The final certificate is then issued within 28 days of this statement (or, within 28 days of the issue of the certificate of making good, or the expiry of the last rectification period, whichever is the latest) (cl 4·14·1). It is worth noting that it has been held that the final certificate can be issued at the same time as the statement, although it would be good practice to allow the contractor time to consider the document (*Penwith District Council v V P Developments*). The final certificate must state the contract sum as adjusted under clause 4·3, which sets out all the deductions and additions to the contract sum (cl 4·14·2). As with interim certificates, the final certificate can be for a negative amount – in other words, it can certify that payment is due from the contractor to the employer.

Penwith District Council v *V P Developments Ltd* [1999] EWHC Technology 231

Penwith employed VP for maintenance works to 91 houses at Hayle. The contract was on JCT80. Practical completion took place on 21 September 1990, and the certificate of making good was issued on 30 October 1991. VP submitted a draft final account on 14 January 1991. Three interim certificates were issued following practical completion, the last one on 10 July 1992. The final certificate was issued on 8 April 1993, and enclosed a document summarising how the figure on the final certificate had been calculated. VP gave notice of arbitration some three years later. It argued that it was not barred by the clause 30·9 conclusiveness provisions as the final certificate had not been valid. The arbitrator found for VP, stating that the intention of the contract was that the contractor should have at least three months to consider the ascertainment of final account referred to in clause 30·6·1. Penwith appealed and His Honour Judge Humphrey Lloyd found that the contract terms required that no minimum period should have elapsed; all the time limits referred to were maxima. He also found that no such term could be implied, 'the 1980 JCT form is a long and complex document and was plainly intended to provide for most conceivable circumstances and to block the many attempts to find gaps in its structures, despite repeated assaults'.

7.45   The final date for payment of the final certificate is 28 days from the due date (cl 4·14·3). As with interim certificates, the final certificate can be for a negative amount – in other words it can certify that payment is due from the contractor to the employer. The final certificate is subject to pay less notice provisions as described above in relation to interim certificates (cl 4·14·4–4·14·6).

Payment when no final certificate is issued

7.46   If no final certificate is issued within the required two-month period, the contractor may send a final payment notice to the employer (cl 4·14·6·1). The notice should state 'what the Contractor considers to be the amount of the final payment due to him under this Contract and the basis on which the sum has been calculated'. Where a final payment notice is given, clause 4·14·6·2 states that 'the final date for payment of the sum specified in it shall for all purposes be regarded as postponed by the same number of days as the number of days after expiry of the 28 day period that the Final Payment Notice is given'. If the employer disagrees with the amount shown on the payment notice, then it may issue a pay less notice under clause 4·14·6·3. The employer is then only obliged to pay the amount shown in the pay less notice.

7.47   In the unlikely event that neither a final certificate nor a payment notice is issued, the contract nevertheless provides that there is a date by which a final payment is due. Clause 4·14·3 states that 'The due date for the final payment shall be the date of issue of the Final Certificate or, if that certificate is not issued within the 28 day period referred to in clause 4·14·1, the last day of that period and, subject to clause 4·14·6, the final date for payment shall be 28 days from its due date'. This provides protection to the contractor in that, even if it does not issue a payment notice, in any subsequent proceedings there will be a reference point from which interest may be calculated, based on the sum which it is later determined should have been paid at that time.

Conclusive effect of final certificate

7.48   The final certificate is conclusive evidence that proper adjustment has been made to the contract sum, and the contractor is prevented from seeking to raise any further claims for extensions of time, or for reimbursement of direct loss and/or expense. It is also conclusive evidence that, where matters have been expressly stated to be for the approval of the contract administrator, they have been approved but, apart from those matters, it does not provide conclusive evidence that any other materials, workmanship, etc. are in accordance with the contract (cl 1·10).

7.49   Both parties have the right to challenge the issue of the final certificate by commencing proceedings within 28 days of its issue. (cl 1·9·2). This right to challenge the final certificate subsequent to its issue does not depend on the issue of any pay less notices or any other challenge (for example, with respect to the final statement, prior to its issue). If dispute resolution proceedings are commenced before the issue of the final certificate, it does not become conclusive of any matters covered until the proceedings are concluded or, if the party which has taken the initial steps then takes no further action for a period of 12 months, then the certificate has the conclusive effect stated (cl 1·9·2). If the proceedings are commenced after the certificate is issued then it is only conclusive with respect to matters that are not challenged in the proceedings (cl 1·9·3).

7.50   After the 28-day period has elapsed there would be little purpose in either party seeking to raise a claim. The bar on raising matters after the 28-day period cannot be extended by the court, as the bar is an evidential bar and not a bar to bringing arbitration proceedings. In other words, arbitration can be commenced, but no evidence can be brought forward.

7.51   The conclusive effect of the final certificate has been the subject of much heated debate over recent years, following the decisions in *Colbart Ltd* v *H Kumar* and *Crown Estates Commissioners* v *John Mowlem*. The JCT has amended the relevant clauses in its contracts, so that it should be possible for the employer to bring a claim regarding work or materials which were not in accordance with the contract following the 28-day cut-off period, provided that they had not been stated to be 'to approval' of the contract administrator somewhere within the contract documents. Despite this, the author occasionally comes across practices which, although working with the new forms, are still implementing a policy of never issuing final certificates, or issuing them with alterations or declarations on their face, all measures adopted in the difficult period immediately following the cases. There is no longer any justification for taking such steps, and indeed they would constitute a breach of contract on the part of the employer, therefore putting the employer at considerable risk. Provided that the contract administrator has taken all steps required by the contract, and has made a competent inspection of the works at the right stage, the certificate must be issued as the contract requires.

Colbart Ltd v H Kumar (1992) 59 BLR 89

Colbart Ltd, a contractor, entered into a contract with Mr Kumar on IFC84 (with Amendments 1 and 2) to carry out work to property belonging to Mr Kumar in south-east London. In November 1990, the contract administrator issued a practical completion certificate, followed one week later by a penultimate certificate and then, three weeks after that, by a certificate of making good defects and a final certificate. Three months after the issue of the penultimate certificate, and six weeks after the final certificate, the contractor commenced proceedings for the amounts certified. As part of the defence to this claim, Mr Kumar asserted that some of the work certified was defective. Clause 4·7 of this edition of IFC84 stated that the final certificate was 'conclusive evidence that where and to the extent that the quality of materials or the standard of workmanship are to be to the reasonable satisfaction of the Architect/the Contract Administrator the same are to such satisfaction'. The judge stated that the conclusive effect extended to items where the standard was inherently a matter for the opinion of the contract administrator. Whether or not the quality of any materials or workmanship was inherently a matter for the opinion of the contract administrator was a question of fact and degree in each case. In this project the defective work which was the cause of the complaint was such an instance, and there was therefore no arguable defence to the contractor's claim.

Crown Estates Commissioners v John Mowlem & Co. Ltd (1994) 70 BLR 1 (CA)

Crown Estates employed Mowlem to construct a commercial development on the site of the former Kensington Palace Barracks. A final certificate was issued on 2 December 1992 and, on 6 April 1993, Crown Estates gave notice of arbitration. It then issued a summons under section 27 of the Arbitration Act 1979 for an order extending the time within which to commence arbitration, in order to validate its notice. In addition to the summons, the judge at first instance was also asked to consider the question of what, if anything, the final certificate was conclusive evidence of, as this would affect what could be raised in the arbitration. The judge issued the order extending time and held that the final certificate was only conclusive as to matters that were expressly stated to be for the satisfaction of the contract administrator. Mowlem appealed and the appeal was allowed. The Court of Appeal stated that clause 30·9·1·1 and 30·9·3 did not limit the time within which arbitration proceedings could be brought, therefore the court had no powers under the Arbitration Act 1979 that could defeat the effect of the certificate. It also held that as all standards and quality of work and materials were inherently matters for the opinion of the contract administrator, the final certificate was conclusive evidence of all such matters.

---

8 Indemnity and insurance

8.1   One of the most important functions of a building contract is to establish a clear allocation of liability for the risks inherent in any construction operation, i.e. the risks of accident, injury and damage to property. Should any unfortunate incidents occur, it is vital that there should be no room for dispute about who is liable for the losses, and that all concerned are clear about what procedural steps must be taken. Ambiguity will only lead to confusion and delays, which will benefit neither party.

8.2   Normally a building contract will set out the specific events for which the contractor is liable, and require the contractor to indemnify the employer in respect of the resultant losses, for example for injury to persons, or damage to neighbouring property. In IC11 these liabilities are allocated under clauses 6·1 and 6·2. These clauses make the contractor liable for, and require indemnification of the employer against, claims for injury to or death of persons, or damage to neighbouring property, which has been caused by the contractor's negligence. The indemnity protects the employer in that if an injured party brings an action against the employer, rather than against the contractor, the latter has agreed to carry the consequences of the claim. In practice, the employer can either join the contractor as co-defendant or bring separate proceedings against the contractor.

8.3   The indemnities given to the employer by the contractor are, in practice, quite worthless if the contractor has insufficient resources to meet the claims. IC11 therefore requires the contractor, under clause 6·4, to carry insurance cover to back up the indemnities required under clauses 6·1 and 6·2.

8.4   In addition to the requirement for insurance against claims arising in respect of persons and property, the contract contains alternative provisions for insurance of the works under clauses 6·7 to 6·11 and Schedule 1. There are also optional provisions requiring the contractor to take out insurance for non-negligent damage to property other than the works (cl 6·5).

Injury to persons and damage to property caused by the negligence of the contractor

8.5   Clause 6·4 requires the contractor to carry insurance to cover injury to persons and damage to property other than the works which arise from the carrying out of the works. The minimum cover required as a contractual obligation is entered in the contract particulars. The contractor must be able to provide evidence that this insurance has been taken out. If the contractor defaults, the employer may take out the insurance and deduct the cost from the contract sum.

8.6   The contractor's liability in respect of personal injury or death of employees is met by an employer's liability policy. This has been compulsory since the Employers' Liability

(Compulsory Insurance) Act 1969. The contractor's liability in respect of third parties (death or personal injury and loss or damage to property including consequential loss) is met by its public liability policy. Insurers advocate insuring for a minimum of £2,000,000 for any one occurrence, although a minimum cover of £250,000 was all that was required under the Finance (No. 2) Act 1975. Liability at common law for claims by third parties is unlimited, and any amount specified in the contract is merely the employer's requirement in the interests of safeguarding against inadequacies, and in no way limits the contractor's liability under clause 6·1.

8.7   Clause 6·4·1·1 requires that the insurance in respect of personal injury or death of any person in a contract of service with the contractor should comply with all relevant legislation, for example, insurance requirements under the Road Traffic Act 1988.

8.8   The contractor is required to insure the indemnities required under clauses 6·1 and 6·2 up to the amount stated in the contract particulars. However, it is recognised in footnote 46 to clause 6·4·1·2 that it may not always be possible to acquire insurance cover which is coextensive with the indemnity required in clauses 6·1 and 6·2. For example, the insurance market has removed gradual pollution from its public liability policies. This in no way affects the contractor's liability and duty to indemnify.

8.9   The liability and duty to indemnify are subject to exceptions. In respect of liability for personal injury or death, this is qualified in that the contractor is not liable where injury or death is caused by an act of the employer, or a person for whom the employer is responsible (cl 6·1).

8.10   In respect of damage to property, the contractor is only liable to the extent that the damage is caused by negligence or breach of statutory duty or other default of 'the Contractor or any of the Contractor's Persons' (cl 6·2). The contractor is therefore liable only for losses caused by its own negligence. It is made clear in clause 6·3·1 that the definition of 'property' excludes the works, up to practical completion, except parts taken over by partial possession. The last sentence of clause 6·2 excludes liability for loss or damage to property caused by a 'Specified Peril' where this is required to be insured under Schedule 1 Option C. This means that, where Option C is applicable, the contractor is not liable for losses insured under that clause and caused by a 'Specified Peril', even where the damage is caused by the contractor's own negligence (*Scottish Special Housing Association* v *Wimpey Construction* and *Scottish and Newcastle plc* v *GD Construction (St Albans) Ltd*). Domestic sub-contractors, however, may be liable for losses caused by their negligence (*BT* v *James Thompson & Sons*). It should be noted, also, that the contractor might remain liable for some consequential losses (*Kruger Tissue* v *Frank Galliers*).

Scottish Special Housing Association v *Wimpey Construction UK Ltd* (1986) 34 BLR 1

Scottish Special Housing Association (SSHA) entered into a contract with Wimpey on JCT63 (1977 edition) to modernise 128 houses in Edinburgh. During the course of the works some of the houses were damaged by fire and it was assumed for the purposes of the case that the fire was caused by the contractor's negligence. Clause 18(2) (the equivalent is cl 6·2 in IC11), which dealt with the contractor's liability for damage to property, was headed by the phrase 'except for such loss and damage as is at the risk of the Employer under … 20(C)' (Insurance Option C in IC11). The court found that this had the effect of exempting the contractor from liability for any loss or damage that was required to be insured under clause 20(C), however caused.

Scottish and Newcastle plc v *GD Construction (St Albans) Ltd* [2003] BLR 131 (CA)

Scottish and Newcastle entered into a contract with GD Construction on IFC84 to carry out refurbishment work to a public house in Reading. During the course of work a fire broke out. There was a trial of a preliminary issue as to whether or not the contractor was liable to the employer for the cost of the repair to the existing structure, and it was assumed, for the purposes of the trial, that the fire was caused by the contractor's negligence. The trial judge found the contractor liable and the contractor appealed. It was held, allowing the appeal, that the combined effect of clauses 6·1·2 and 6·3·1C was that the contractor was not liable for these losses. The express linkage between these two clauses was considered key to reaching this decision.

British Telecommunications plc v *James Thompson & Sons (Engineers) Ltd* [1999] BLR 35 (HL)

James Thompson was a sub-contractor on a refurbishment project for BT being undertaken on a JCT80 form of contract. A fire broke out in the roof area while the sub-contractor was carrying out its work. The court found that the relevant clauses had the same effect as the equivalent clauses considered in *SSHA* v *Wimpey*. However, it decided that domestic sub-contractors remained under a duty of care to prevent such losses, and James Thompson was therefore liable to BT under the tort of negligence. The court considered that the wording of clause 22·3, which required the joint names policies to waive the rights of subrogation against nominated but not domestic sub-contractors, should be taken into account in considering whether a duty of care existed. The fact that BT was indemnified by the clause 22C insurers (Insurance Option C in IC11) even if the fire were to be caused by the sub-contractor, was insufficient to prevent the imposition of the duty.

Kruger Tissue (Industrial) Ltd v *Frank Galliers Ltd* (1998) 57 Con LR 1

Damage was caused to the existing building and works by fire, assumed for the purposes of the case to be the result of the negligence of the contractor or sub-contractor. The construction work being carried out was on a JCT80 form. The employer brought a claim for loss of profits, increased cost of working and consultants' fees, all of which were consequential losses. Judge John Hicks decided that the employer's duty to insure for 'the full cost of reinstatement, repair or replacement of the existing structure and the works under clause 22C (and therefore contractor's exemption from liability under clause 20·2), did not include such consequential losses'. A claim could therefore be brought against the contractor for these losses.

Damage to property not caused by the negligence of the contractor

8.11   The liability for damage to adjoining buildings where there has been no negligence on the part of the contractor is not covered under clause 6·2. Subsidence or vibration resulting from the carrying out of the works might cause such damage, even though the contractor has taken reasonable care. This is a risk which may be quite high in certain projects, such as on tight urban sites or in close proximity to old buildings. In such cases it may be advisable to take out a special policy for the benefit of the employer.

8.12   In IC11 there is an optional provision for this type of insurance under clause 6·5·1. If it is anticipated that the main contractor may be required to take out this insurance, the correct deletion must be made in the contract particulars, and the amount of cover entered. The contract administrator must then instruct the contractor to take out the policy, after confirming with the employer that the policy is required. The cost is added to the contract sum. The policy must be in joint names and placed with insurers approved by the employer. The policy and receipt are to be deposited with the employer.

8.13   This insurance is usually expensive, and subject to a great many exceptions. If it is required, then the policy needs to be effective at the start of the site operations when demolition, excavation, etc. are carried out. The text of clause 6·5 was revised in 1996 to take account of the wording of model exclusions compiled by the Association of British Insurers. The policy should be checked by the employer's insurance advisers to ensure that any exclusions correlate with clause 6·5 and that the policy provides the cover that the clause requires.

Insurance of the works

8.14   There are three alternative clauses covering insurance of the works, and the applicable clause should be entered in the contract particulars (note there is no need to delete clauses in the form itself). In all cases, the policies are to be in joint names, and cover must be maintained until practical completion of the works, or termination, if this should occur earlier. All three alternatives are for joint names policies. The 'Joint Names Policy' definition was reworded in 1996 to make clear the intention that, under the policy, the insurer does not have a right of subrogation to recover any of the monies from either of the named parties. The policies must also either cover named sub-contractors or include a waiver of any rights of subrogation against them (cl 6·9·1). With the exception of joint names policies under Schedule 1 paragraph C·1, the requirements for recognition or waiver must apply also to domestic sub-contractors.

8.15   Insurance Option A and Option B cover the insurance of new building work and require 'All Risks' cover under joint names policies. A definition of 'All Risks' is given in clause 6·8 and refers to 'any physical loss or damage to work executed and Site Materials and against the reasonable cost of the removal and disposal of debris'. There is also a list of exclusions, which includes the cost necessary to repair, replace or rectify property which is defective, loss or damage due to defective design, loss or damage arising from war and hostilities and 'Excepted Risks' (except as provided by terrorism cover). Footnote 51 explains that cover should not be reduced beyond the exclusions set out in the definitions. It also points out that 'all Risks' cover that includes the risk of defective design, although not required, may be available. If the policy provided is likely to differ in any way from the requirements in the contract, this must be discussed and agreed before the contract is entered into. Even in a so-called 'All Risks' insurance policy there may be further exclusions, and the employer's insurance advisers should carefully check the wording of each policy.

8.16   Option A insurance is taken out by the contractor and is to be for the full reinstatement value of the works, including professional fees, to the extent entered in the contract particulars. The contractor is responsible for keeping the works fully covered and, in the event of under-insurance, will be liable for any shortfall in recovery from the insurers.

8.17   Option B insurance is taken out by the employer, and must be for the full reinstatement value of the works, including professional fees. The employer is responsible for keeping the works fully covered and, in the event of under-insurance, will be liable for any shortfall.

8.18   Option C is applicable where work is being carried out to existing buildings. It includes two insurances, both taken out by the employer. The existing structure and contents must be insured against 'Specified Perils' as defined in clause 6·8 (Option C:C·1). New works in, or extensions to, existing buildings must be covered by an 'All Risks' insurance policy (Option C:C·2).

Action following damage to the works

8.19   The procedure is similar under Insurance Options A (A·4), B (B·3) and C (C·4). The contractor must notify the contract administrator and the employer in writing of the details of the damage as soon as possible. Although the contract does not require it, clearly the contractor or employer, depending on who has taken out the policy, should also inform the insurers immediately on becoming aware of the damage. After any necessary inspection has been made by the insurers, the contractor is then obliged to make good the damage and continue with the works. Under all three clauses, the contractor authorises the payment of all monies due under the insurance policy to be made directly to the employer.

8.20   All three options state that 'the occurrence of such loss or damage shall be disregarded in computing any amounts payable to the Contractor' (A·4·2, B·3·2 and C·4·2). Interim certificates that have already been issued and the amounts paid or due under them are, of course, not affected by the occurrence of the damage. In addition, any work that was completed after the most recent interim certificate, but was then subsequently damaged, should also be included in the next interim certificate.

8.21   Under Option A, the contractor must take out insurance for the full reinstatement value of the works, plus a percentage to cover professional fees if this is required in the contract particulars (A·1). This money, less the portion of it to cover professional fees, should be paid by instalments under certificates as the work is carried out (A·4·4). The sums are not added to the contract sum and the reinstatement work is kept distinct by issuing separate certificates (often referred to as 'reinstatement certificates') which cover only that work, at the same intervals as the normal interim certificates. If the amount paid by the insurers is less than it costs the contractor to rebuild the works, the contractor is not entitled to any additional payment (A·4·6). The risk of any under-insurance therefore lies with the contractor.

8.22   Under Options B and C, where the insurance is taken by the employer, the rebuilding work is treated as if it were a variation under clause 3·11 (cl B·3·5 and C·4·5), therefore the contractor is less at risk and the employer will have to bear any shortfall in the monies paid out. Under clause 2·20·9 the contractor is entitled to an extension of time for delay caused by loss or damage due to one or more of the specified perils. In addition, as the work is treated as a variation, the contractor may be entitled to an extension of time and loss and/or expense under clauses 2·20·1 and 4·18·1. In all cases the entitlement appears to extend even to cases where the damage was caused by the contractor's negligence.

8.23   Under Option C, either party is given the right to terminate the employment of the contractor 'if it is just and equitable' to do so (C·4·4). This might arise, for example, where an existing structure to which work is being carried out has been completely destroyed, and it would be quite unreasonable to expect the contractor to rebuild it. If the contract is terminated, the provisions of clause 8·12 apply. It should be noted that this right is in addition to the right under clause 8·11 of either party to terminate the contractor's employment should the works be suspended for a period of two months due to loss or damage caused by a specified peril (cl 8·11·1·3).

The Joint Fire Code

8.24   The Joint Fire Code (cl 6·12 to 6·15) is designed to reduce the incidence of fire on construction sites. It is an optional provision but, as compliance with the code may reduce the cost of some insurance policies, its inclusion should be carefully considered. If it is included, both parties undertake to comply with the code and ensure that those employed by them also comply.

8.25   If a breach of the Fire Code occurs, the insurers may give notice to either the employer or the contractor of remedial measures they require and the dates by which these must be put into effect. If either party receives such a notice, they must copy it to the other, and the employer must send a copy to the contract administrator (cl 6·14·1). If the notice sets out measures which conform to the contractor's existing obligations under the contract, then the contractor should put the measures in place (cl 6·14·1·1). If the contractor does not comply with the notice within seven days, the employer may employ and pay others to effect such compliance (cl 6·14·2).

8.26   Where the remedial measures in the notice constitute a variation to the contract, the contract administrator must issue instructions as necessary to enable compliance. In an emergency, i.e. where the insurer's notice requires immediate compliance, the contractor should take such steps as are reasonably necessary to achieve such compliance and should inform the contract administrator immediately of the position (cl 6·14·1·2).

Terrorism cover

8.27   Under clause 6·10, the contractor (where Insurance Option A applies) or the employer (where Insurance Options B or C apply), is required to take out terrorism cover. This can be done either as an extension to the joint names policy or as a separate joint names policy, and must be taken out in the same amount and for the required period of the joint names policy. 'Terrorism Cover' is defined as 'Pool Re Cover or other insurance against loss or damage to work executed and Site Materials (and/or, for the purposes of clause 6·11·1, to an existing structure and/or its contents) caused by or resulting from terrorism' (cl 6·8). 'Pool Re Cover' is also a defined term, and stands for 'such insurance against loss or damage to work executed and Site Materials caused by or resulting from terrorism as is from time to time generally available from insurers who are members of the Pool Reinsurance Company Limited scheme or of any similar successor scheme' (cl 6·8). Although there have been difficulties in the past in obtaining such cover, at the time of writing, the insurance market is prepared to cover terrorism risks. If cover is not available, or is likely to differ from the contractual requirements, then, as with insurance generally, the details must be agreed before the contract is signed.

8.28   If, however, the insurers named in the joint names policy decide to withdraw this cover and notify either party, that party must immediately notify the other that terrorism cover has ceased (cl 6·11·1) The employer must then decide whether or not it wishes to continue with the works, and notify the contractor accordingly (cl 6·11·2). If the employer decides to terminate the contractor's employment, the provisions of clauses 8·12·2 to 8·12·5 apply (cl 6·11·4, see Chapter 9). Otherwise, should any damage be caused by terrorism, the contractor is required to make good the damage and the related work is treated as a variation (cl 6·11·5).

Professional indemnity insurance

8.29   Under ICD11 the contractor is required to carry professional indemnity insurance (cl 6·16). The level and amount of cover must be inserted in the contract particulars – if no level is inserted it will be 'the aggregate amount for any one period of insurance', and if no amount is stated no insurance will be required. There is a provision for inserting a level of cover for pollution or contamination claims. In addition if the expiry period is to be 12 years from practical completion then this must be indicated, or otherwise the period will be six years. The insurance must be taken out immediately following the execution of the contract, and maintained until the end of the stipulated expiry period. The contractor must provide evidence of the insurance if required (cl 6·16·3).

Other insurance

8.30   There remain risks to the employer that are not covered by the IC11 insurance provisions. For example, if the contractor is caused delay by one of the specified perils, an extension of time would normally be awarded under clause 2·19·1 and the employer will not be able to claim liquidated damages from the contractor for that period. There will therefore be a loss to the employer as a result. Should the employer wish to be insured against this loss of liquidated damages, then special provisions must be made, as there is nothing in IC11 which deals with such loss. The possible risks should be explained to the employer, but it should be noted that there are often problems with such insurance as liquidated damages are payable without proof and, traditionally, insurers only pay on proof of actual loss. As a result, only one or two firms are currently willing to offer cover and the price tends to be high.

8.31   There are other forms of insurance that are not covered by IC11 which the employer might wish to consider. The employer is the party best-placed to assess possible loss. Where there are likely to be business or other economic losses, then these can be covered, albeit at a price. It is also possible to insure against defects occurring in the buildings by means of project-related insurance. This insurance is still relatively expensive and limited to a ten-year 'decennial' loss. Irrespective of blame, it means that money is available for remedying the defects which will occur most often in the first eight years of the life of a building. Project-related insurance should include subrogation waiver, and in no way reduces the need for professional indemnity cover.

The contract administrator's role in insurance

8.32   The contract administrator has a duty to explain the provisions of the contract to the employer, and should therefore have a working knowledge of insurance matters, although the contract administrator would not be expected to be an expert. The choice of the appropriate option for insuring 'the Works' is particularly important, and advice must be given to the employer concerning the consequences. In addition, the contract administrator will monitor the actions of the parties with respect to the insurance clauses, even though, for the most part, the insurance provisions are dealt with directly between the employer and contractor. The contract administrator should be alert to the need for swift action should loss or damage occur, and may be required to attend an inspection by the insurers, or to supply information.

8.33   The employer should take advice from its own insurance experts concerning the suitability and wording of any policies. The contract administrator is primarily a channel of communication, and although a check should be carried out on wording to see that no undesirable exceptions or restrictions exist that might affect the carrying out of the works, the main responsibility should rest with the employer and the employer's broker or insurance advisers.

8.34   Where the insurance requirements of the contract cannot be matched by effective cover, then the employer should seek expert advice. For example, the building might be special and uninsurable, or the employer might not wish to have insurance, etc. Decisions in such situations will also have implications for contractors and sub-contractors, and expert advice must be sought.

9 Default and termination

9.1   Given the complexity and unpredictability of construction operations, it would be unlikely that a project could proceed to completion without breaches of the contractual terms by one party or another. This is recognised by most construction forms, which usually include provisions to deal with foreseeable situations. These provisions avoid arguments developing or the need to bring legal proceedings as the parties have agreed in advance machinery for dealing with the breach. A clear example of this is the provisions for liquidated damages – the contractor is technically in breach if the project is not completed by the contractual date, but all the consequences and procedures for dealing with this are set out in the contract itself. However, some breaches may have such significant consequences that the other party may prefer not to continue with the contract, and for these more serious breaches the contract contains provisions for terminating the employment of the contractor.

Repudiation or termination

9.2   In any contract, where the behaviour of one party makes it difficult or impossible for the other to carry out its contractual obligations, the injured party might allege prevention of performance and sue either for damages or a *quantum meruit*. This could occur in construction, for example, where the employer refuses to allow access to part of the site.

9.3   Where it is impossible to expect further performance from a party, then the injured party may claim that the contract has been repudiated. Repudiation occurs when one party makes it clear that they no longer intend to be bound by the provisions of the contract. This intention might be expressly stated, or implied by the party's behaviour.

9.4   Most JCT contracts include termination clauses, which provide for the effective termination of the employment of the contractor in circumstances which may amount to, or which may fall short of, repudiation. It should be noted that the termination is of the contractor's employment under the contract, and is not termination of the contract itself. This means that the parties remain bound by its provisions, and can bring actions for losses suffered through breach of its terms.

9.5   If repudiation occurs, it is unnecessary to invoke a termination clause, since the injured party can accept the repudiation and bring the contract to an end. However, the termination provisions are useful in setting out the exact circumstances, procedures and consequences of the termination of employment. These procedures must be followed with great caution because, if they are not administered strictly in accordance with the terms of the contract, this in itself could amount to a repudiation of the contract. This, in turn, might give the other party the right to treat the contract as at an end and claim damages.

9.6   Termination can be initiated by the employer (cl 8·4) in the event of specified defaults by the contractor, such as suspending the works or failing to comply with the CDM Regulations or in the event of the insolvency of the contractor. Termination can be initiated by the contractor (cl 8·9) in the event of specified defaults by the employer, such as failure to pay the amount due on a certificate or where specified events result in the suspension of work beyond a period to be entered in the contract particulars. Termination might also follow the insolvency of the employer. In the event of neutral causes, which bring about the suspension of the uncompleted works for the period listed in the contract particulars, the right of termination can be exercised by either party (cl 8·11).

Termination by the employer

9.7   The contract provides for termination by the employer under stated circumstances. IC11 expressly states that the right to terminate the contractor's employment is 'without prejudice to any other rights and remedies' (cl 8·3·1). Termination can be initiated by the employer in the event of specified defaults by the contractor occurring prior to practical completion (cl 8·4·1), the insolvency of the contractor (cl 8·5) or corruption (cl 8·6). (Note that clause 8·6 defines corruption as an offence under the Bribery Act 2010 or, where the employer is a local authority, particular acts which are an offence under the Local Government Act 1972.)

9.8   The procedures as set out in the contract must be followed exactly, especially those concerning the issue of notices (see Figure 16). If default occurs, the contract administrator should issue a warning notice of 'specified default or defaults' (cl 8·4·1). If the default continues for 14 days from receipt of the notice, then the employer may terminate the employment of the contractor by the issue of a further notice within 21 days from the expiry of the 14 days (cl 8·4·2). If the contractor ends the default, or if the employer gives no further notice, and the contractor then repeats the default, the employer may terminate 'within a reasonable time after such repetition' (cl 8·4·3). The employer must still give a notice of termination, but no further warning is required from the contract administrator. There appears to be no time limit on the repetition of the default. These notices must be given by the means set out in clause 1·7·4, i.e. 'by hand or sent by Recorded Signed for or Special Delivery post' (cl 8·2·3). It should be noted that this is not the same as the older wording 'actual delivery', so it is unlikely that fax or email would be acceptable as in the case of *Construction Partnership* v *Leek Developments*.

Construction Partnership UK Ltd v *Leek Developments Ltd* [2006] CILL 2357 TCC

On an IFC98 contract, a notice of determination was delivered by fax, but not by hand or by special delivery or recorded delivery. (A letter had been sent by normal post but it was unclear whether or not it had been received.) Clause 7·1 required actual delivery of notices of default and determination, and the contractor disputed whether the faxed notice was valid. The court therefore had to decide what 'actual delivery' meant. It decided that it meant what it says: 'Delivery simply means transmission by an appropriate means so that it is received'. In this case, it was agreed that the fax had been received, therefore the notice complied with the clause. The CILL editors state that 'on a practical level, this judgement is quite important' because it had previously been assumed that 'actual delivery' meant physical delivery by hand. In their view, email could be considered an appropriate method of delivery, although that was not decided in the case.

Figure 16 Termination by the employer

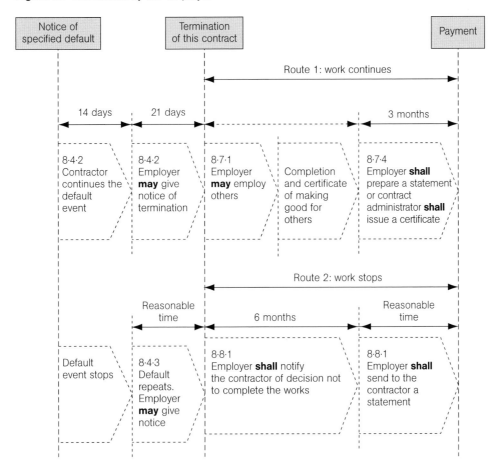

9.9　The grounds for termination by the employer must be clearly established and expressed. The contract clearly states that termination must not be exercised unreasonably or vexatiously (cl 8·2·1). Under clause 8·4·1·1 suspension of the work must be whole and substantial, and 'without reasonable cause'. However, the contractor might find 'reasonable cause' in any of the matters referred to in clause 4·18. An exercise of the right to suspend work under clause 4·13 would not be cause for termination, provided that it had been exercised in accordance with the terms of the contract.

Specified defaults

9.10　The specified defaults which may give rise to termination are that the contractor:

- wholly or substantially suspends the carrying out of the works without reasonable cause (cl 8·4·1·1);

- 'fails to proceed regularly and diligently' (cl 8·4·1·2);

- refuses or neglects to comply with a written instruction requiring the contractor to remove defective work (cl 8·4·1·3);

- fails to comply with clause 7·1 (assignment), clause 3·5 (sub-contracting) and clause 3·7 (named persons) (cl 8·4·1·4);

- and fails to comply with the contractual provisions of the CDM Regulations (cl 8·4·1·5). Generally speaking, the default would have to be serious to justify termination, although any failure to comply with the CDM provisions which would put the employer at risk of action by the authorities would be sufficient.

9.11   The default that the contractor 'fails to proceed regularly and diligently' (cl 8·4·1·2) is notoriously difficult to establish, and although meticulous records will help, contract administrators are often understandably reluctant to issue the first warning notice. It means more than simply falling behind any submitted programme, even to such an extent that it is quite clear the project will finish considerably behind time. However, something less than a complete cessation of work on site would be sufficient grounds.

9.12   In the case of *London Borough of Hounslow* v *Twickenham Garden Developments*, for example, the contract administrator's notice was strongly attacked by the defendants. In a more recent case, however, the contract administrator was found negligent because it failed to issue a notice (*West Faulkner Associates* v *London Borough of Newham*). It should be remembered that without the first 'warning notice' issued by the contract administrator the employer cannot issue the termination notice.

London Borough of Hounslow v *Twickenham Garden Developments* (1970) 7 BLR 81

The London Borough of Hounslow entered into a contract with Twickenham Garden Developments to carry out sub-structure works at Heston and Isleworth in Middlesex. The contract was on JCT63. Work on the contract stopped for approximately eight months due to a strike. After work resumed, the architect issued a notice of default stating that the contractor had failed to proceed regularly and diligently and that, unless there was an appreciable improvement, the contract would be determined. The employer then proceeded to determine the contractor's employment. The contractor disputed the validity of the notices and the determination, and refused to stop work and leave the site. Hounslow applied to the court for an injunction to remove the contractor. The judge emphasised that an injunction was a serious remedy and that, before he could grant one, there had to be clear and indisputable evidence of the merits of Hounslow's case. The evidence put before him, which showed a significant drop in the amounts of monthly certificates and numbers of workers on site, failed to provide this.

West Faulkner Associates v *London Borough of Newham* (1992) 61 BLR 81

West Faulkner Associates were architects engaged by the London Borough of Newham for the refurbishment of a housing estate consisting of several blocks of flats. The residents of the estate were evacuated from their flats in stages to make way for the contractor, Moss, which, it had been agreed, would carry out the work according to a programme of phased possession and completion, with each block taking nine weeks. Moss fell behind the programme almost immediately. However, Moss had a large workforce on the site and continually promised to revise its programme and working methods to address the problems of lateness, poor quality work and unsafe working practices that were drawn to its attention on numerous occasions by the architect. In reality, Moss remained completely disorganised, and there was no apparent improvement. The architect took the advice of quantity surveyors that the grounds of failing to proceed regularly and diligently would be difficult to prove, and decided not to issue a notice. As a consequence, Newham was unable to issue a notice of determination, had to negotiate a settlement with the contractor and dismissed the architect, which then brought a claim for its fees.

The judge decided that the architect was in breach of contract in failing to give proper consideration to the use of the determination provisions. In his judgment, he stated that 'regularly and diligently' should be construed together and in essence they mean simply that the contractors must go about their work in such a way as to achieve their contractual obligations. 'This requires them to plan their work, to lead and manage their workforce, to provide sufficient and proper materials and to employ competent tradesmen, so that the Works are carried out to an acceptable standard and that all time, sequence and other provisions are fulfilled' (Judge Newey at page 139).

Insolvency of the contractor

9.13 Insolvency is the inability to pay debts as they become due for payment. Insolvent individuals may be declared bankrupt. Insolvent companies may be dealt with in a number of ways, depending upon the circumstances: for example, by voluntary liquidation (in which the company resolves to wind itself up); compulsory liquidation (under which the company is wound up by a court order); administrative receivership (a procedure to assist the rescue of a company under appointed receivers); an administration order (a court order given in response to a petition, again with the aim of rescue rather than liquidation, and managed by an appointed receiver); or voluntary arrangement (in which the company agrees terms with creditors over payment of debts). IC11 sets out a full definition of the term 'Insolvent' for the purposes of the contract at clause 8·1. Procedures for dealing with insolvency are mainly subject to the Insolvency Act 1986 and the Insolvency Rules 1996 (SI 1996/1925). Under these provisions, the person authorised to oversee statutory insolvency procedures is termed an 'insolvency practitioner'.

9.14 Under IC11, the contractor must notify the employer in writing in the event of liquidation or insolvency (cl 8·5·2). Termination is not automatic, however. This is to allow the appointed insolvency practitioner time to come up with a rescue package, if possible. It is usually in the employer's interest to have the works completed with as little additional delay and cost as possible, and a breathing space might allow all possibilities to be explored. During this period, the contract states that 'clauses 8·7·3 to 8·7·5 and (if relevant) clause 8·8 shall apply as if such notice had been given' (cl 8·5·3·1). This means that even if no notice of termination is given, the employer is under no obligation to make further payment except as provided under those clauses (see paragraph 9.19). The contractor is relieved of the obligation to 'carry out and complete the Works' (cl 8·5·3·2). The employer may then take reasonable steps to ensure that the site, works and materials are secure and protected, and the contractor may not hinder such measures (cl 8·5·3·3).

9.15 There are three options for completing the project. The first allows for arrangements to be made for the contractor to continue and complete the works. Unless the insolvency practitioner has been able to arrange resource backing, this may not be a realistic option.

If practical completion is near, however, and money is due to the contractor, it can be advantageous to allow completion under the control of the insolvency practitioner.

9.16 Under the second option, another contractor may be novated to complete the works. On a 'true novation', the substitute contractor takes over all the original obligations and benefits (including completion to time and within the contract sum). More likely is the third option, 'conditional novation', whereby the contract completion date, etc. would be subject to renegotiation, and the substitute contractor would probably want to disclaim liability for that part of the work undertaken by the original contractor.

9.17 Deciding on which of the options would best serve the interests of all the parties is a matter to be resolved by the employer, with advice from the contract administrator and the insolvency practitioner. There might be merit in adopting one particular course of action, or there might be advantages in taking a more pragmatic approach. For example, it may prove expeditious to continue initially with the original contractor under an interim arrangement until such time as novation can be arranged or a completion contract negotiated.

Consequences of termination

9.18 If the employer exercises its right to terminate under clause 8·4, 8·5 or 8·6, then the only way to achieve completion will be through the appointment of a new contractor of the employer's choice. The contract gives the employer the right to employ others under clause 8·7·1 to complete the works. This would include making good any defects in the work already carried out and, in the case of ICD11, to complete the designed portion. A completion contract might result from negotiation or competitive tender. The employer will have the right to use any temporary buildings, plant, etc. on site which are not owned by the original contractor, subject to the consent of the owner (cl 8·7·1).

9.19 Following termination, clause 8·7·3 states that 'no further sums shall become due to the Contractor … other than any amount that may become due to him under clause 8·7·5 or 8·8·2'. It also states that the employer will not need to make any payments that have already become due to the extent that a pay less notice has been given (cl 8·7·3·1) or where the contractor has become insolvent (cl 8·7·3·2). This reflects section 111(10) of the HGCRA as amended, and the judgment in *Melville Dundas* v *George Wimpey*. It should be noted, however, that the employer may still be obliged to pay amounts awarded by an adjudicator (*Ferson* v *Levolux*). A notional final account must be set out, stating what is owed or owing, either in a statement prepared by the employer or in a contract administrator's certificate (cl 8·7·4). This must be done within three months after the completion of the works, which allows the employer a period to assess its losses due to the termination. The net amount shown on the account must be paid by the contractor to the employer or, as the case may be, by the employer to the contractor (cl 8·7·5), although in practice the former is the more likely outcome.

Melville Dundas Ltd v *George Wimpey UK Ltd* [2007] 1 WLR 1136 (HL)

On a contract let on WCD98, the contractor had gone into receivership, entitling the employer to determine the contractor's employment. The contractor had applied for an interim payment on 2 May

2003, the final date for payment was 16 May (14 days after application), and the determination was effective on 30 May. The contractor claimed the payment on the basis that no withholding notice had been issued. By a majority of three to two, the House of Lords decided that the employer was not obliged to make any further payment. It was accepted that, under WCD98, interim payments were not contractually payable after determination and the House of Lords held that this was not inconsistent with the payment provisions of the HGCRA 1996. Although the Act requires that the contractor should be entitled to payment in the absence of a notice, this did not mean that that entitlement had to be maintained after the contractor had become insolvent, i.e. it was not inconsistent to construe that the effect of the determination was that the payment was no longer due. The Act was concerned with the balance of interests between payer and payee, and to construe it otherwise would give a benefit to the contractor's creditors against the interests of the employer, something which the Act did not intend.

Ferson Contractors Ltd v *Levolux AT Ltd* [2003] BLR 118

Ferson was the contractor and Levolux the sub-contractor on a GC/Works sub-contract. A dispute arose regarding Levolux's second application for payment; £56,413 was claimed but only £4,753 was paid. A withholding notice was issued which specified the amount but not the reason for withholding it. Levolux brought a claim to adjudication, and the adjudicator decided that the notice did not comply with section 111 of the HGCRA 1996, and that Ferson should pay the whole amount. Ferson refused to pay and Levolux sought enforcement of the decision. Prior to the adjudication, Levolux had suspended work and Ferson, maintaining that the suspension was unlawful, had determined the contract. It now maintained that, due to clause 29, which stated that 'all sums of money that may be due or accruing due from the contractor's side to the sub-contractors shall cease to be due or accrue due' they did not have to pay this amount. The CA upheld the decision of the judge of first instance that the amount should be paid: 'The contract must be construed so as to give effect to the intent of Parliament'.

9.20   One of the consequences of termination is that it often takes time for the contractor to effect an orderly withdrawal from site, and for the employer to establish the amounts outstanding before final payment. Should the employer decide not to continue with the construction of the works after termination, the employer is required to notify the contractor in writing within six months of that notice (cl 8·8). Within two months of the notification (or within six months of termination, if no work is carried out and no notice issued) the employer must send the contractor a statement of the value of the works and losses suffered as required under clause 8·8.

Termination by the contractor

9.21   The contractor has a reciprocal right to terminate its own employment in the event of specified defaults of the employer (cl 8·9·1), or specified suspension events (cl 8·9·2) or insolvency of the employer (cl 8·10). The specified suspension events must have resulted in the suspension of the whole of the uncompleted works for the continuous period stated in the contract particulars. In the case of specified defaults or suspension events a notice is required, which must specify the default or event. If the default or event continues for 14 days from receipt of the notice, the contractor may terminate the employment by a further notice up to 21 days from the expiry of the 14 days (cl 8·9·3) (see Figure 17). Alternatively, if the employer ends the default or the suspension event ceases, and the

Figure 17 Termination by the contractor

```
┌─────────────────┐          ┌─────────────────┐     ┌─────────────┐          ┌─────────────┐
│   Notice of     │          │   Termination   │     │    Final    │          │   Payment   │
│ specified default/s │      │ of this contract │    │   account   │          │             │
└─────────────────┘          └─────────────────┘     └─────────────┘          └─────────────┘
```

| 14 days | 21 days | Reasonable time | 28 days |

8·9·3
Employer
continues the
default
event

8·9·3
Contractor
may give
notice of
termination
to the
employer

8·12·3
Contractor **shall**
prepare an
account

8·12·5
Employer **shall**
pay the
contractor

Reasonable time

Default
event
ceases

8·9·4
Employer
repeats
default.
Contractor
may give
notice

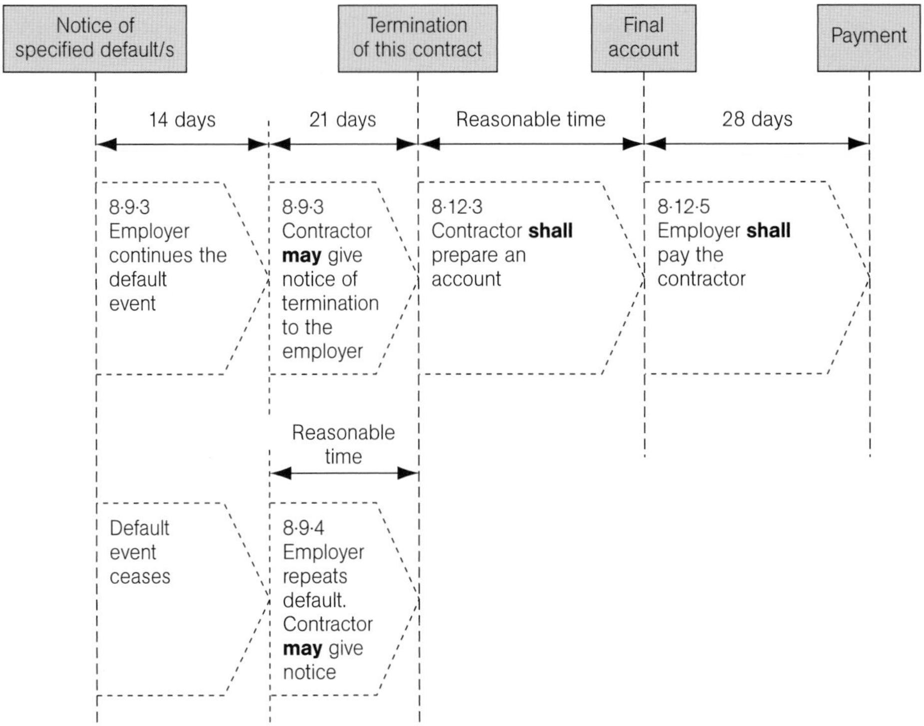

contractor gives no further notice, should the employer repeat the default the contractor may terminate 'within a reasonable time after such repetition' (cl 8·9·4). These notices must be given by the means set out in clause 1·7·4, and not for example by fax or email, as discussed at paragraph 9.8.

9.22   The grounds differ from those that give the employer the right to terminate. They include failure to pay an amount properly due on a certificate, obstruction of the issue of a certificate and failure to comply with the contractual provisions relating to the CDM Regulations. There are also matters which relate directly to the duties of the contract administrator, where, for example, the carrying out of the whole or substantially the whole of the works is suspended as a consequence of an instruction relating to inconsistencies, variations or postponement (cl 8·9·2·1), or due to any 'impediment, prevention or default' of the employer or contract administrator (cl 8·9·2·2), but only if the instruction or default was not necessitated by some negligence or default of the contractor. The contractor may also terminate if the works are suspended through delay by persons engaged directly by the employer, or failure by the employer to give ingress to or egress from the site.

9.23   Termination by the contractor is optional in the case of the employer's bankruptcy or insolvency (cl 8·10·1). The contractor must issue a notice and termination would take effect from the receipt of the notice.

9.24   Following termination under clause 8·9 or 8·10, the contract states that no further sums become due to the contractor otherwise than provided for by that clause (cl 8·12·1). The contractor is required to remove tools etc. from the site and to provide the employer with a copy of documents (cl 8·12·2). The contractor then prepares an account as soon as is reasonably practicable setting out the total value of the work at the date of termination, plus other costs relating to the termination as set out in clause 8·12·3. These may include such items as the cost of removal and any direct loss and/or damage consequent upon termination. The contractor is, in effect, indemnified against any damages that may be caused as a result of the termination.

Termination by either the employer or the contractor

9.25   Either party has the right to terminate the contractor's employment if the carrying out of the works is wholly or substantially suspended for the period inserted in the contract particulars (if none is stated this is two months) due to force majeure, loss or damage to the works caused the specified perils, civil commotion or terrorism, or the exercise by the Government of a statutory power, or a contract administrator's instruction issued as a result of negligence or default of a local authority or statutory undertaker executing work solely in pursuance of its statutory obligations (cl 8·11·1). The right of the contractor to terminate in the event of a specified peril is limited by the proviso that the event must not have been caused by the contractor's negligence (cl 8·11·2).

9.26   Notice may be given by either party and the employment of the contractor will be terminated seven days after receipt of the notice, unless the suspension ceases within seven days after the date of the receipt of that notice. (These notices must be given by the means set out in clause 1·7·4, as discussed at paragraph 9.8.) If the cessation does not stop after this period, the party may then, by further notice, terminate the contract (cl 8·11·1, see Figure 18). Following termination, clauses 8·12·1 (no further sums become due) and 8·12·2 (removal of tools etc. and supply of documents) apply. An account is then

Figure 18 Termination by either party

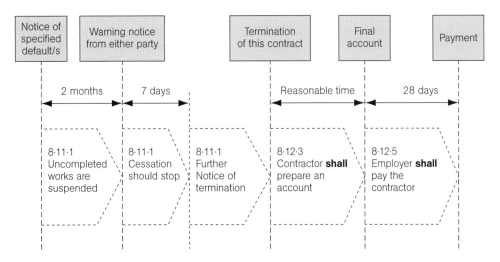

prepared in the same format as for termination by the contractor (cl 8·12·3, see paragraph 9.19), except that in this case amounts relating to direct loss and/or damage to the contractor are only included where they result from a specified peril caused by the employer's negligence.

Termination of the employment of a named person

9.27   The contractor is responsible for taking action with respect to termination of the employment of named persons as sub-contractors. The contract states that the employment of a named person must not be terminated other than through the operation of clauses 7·4 to 7·6 of ICSub/NAM/C, and that the contractor must not bring the sub-contract to an end through acceptance of the repudiation of the sub-contract (Schedule 2:6). The reason for this requirement is that, once the named sub-contract has been terminated, the contractor is required to take steps to recover from the sub-contractor any additional amounts payable to the contractor by the employer as a result of the termination (Schedule 2:10·2·1). If the contractor has not followed the provisions of the sub-contract exactly, the chances of recovery of these losses would be greatly reduced.

9.28   The contractor must advise the contract administrator of any events which might give rise to termination of the named sub-contract. In some circumstances this may give the contract administrator the opportunity to make some investigations and assess in advance the possible alternative courses of action should termination occur.

9.29   The contractor must notify the contract administrator as soon as the contract has been terminated. The contract administrator must then issue instructions which may either name another person to execute the work, require the contractor to complete the work, or omit the outstanding work (Schedule 2:7). The consequences of the termination then depend on whether the sub-contractor was originally named in the contract documents, contract bills/specification/work schedules, or named in an instruction relating to a provisional sum.

9.30   If the sub-contractor was originally named in the tender documents, then an instruction naming a replacement is treated as an event which may be grounds for an extension of time, but not as a matter giving rise to direct loss and/or expense (Schedule 2:8·1). The contract sum is to be adjusted by the difference between the price of the first named sub-contractor for the outstanding work and the price of the replacement, although any amounts in the price of the replacement sub-contractor which cover the correction of defective work are not to be added to the contract sum. The effect of this is that the contractor remains responsible for any defective work carried out by the original named person. An instruction omitting the work, or requiring the contractor to carry out the work, is treated as a variation under clause 5·3, and an event which may give rise to an extension of time and to an award of direct loss and/or expense.

9.31   If the termination relates to a sub-contractor named under an instruction relating to a provisional sum, then the contract administrator's instruction is treated as a further instruction under the provisional sum, and therefore one which may give rise to an adjustment of the contract sum, an extension of time and to an award of direct loss and/or expense (Schedule 2:9). The contract administrator should be careful not to delay unreasonably in issuing instructions following a termination, as this could also be grounds for a claim for extension of time under clause 2·20·2·1, direct loss and/or expense under clause 4·18·2·1, and under exceptional circumstances could even lead to termination under clause 8·11·1·2.

9.32 If the employment of a named sub-contractor is terminated other than in accordance with the contractual provisions, then the contract administrator is still required to issue instructions as described above, but the contract states that these will not result in any right to an extension of time or to direct loss and/or expense, and that no adjustment will be made to the contract sum except if application of the contractual provisions would result in a reduction (Schedule 2:10). The effect of this is to place the entire risk of the consequences of such a termination on the shoulders of the contractor.

10 Dispute resolution

10.1   IC11 refers to five methods of dispute resolution: negotiation; mediation; adjudication; arbitration; and legal proceedings. One of these methods, adjudication, is a statutory right, and if one party wishes to use this method, the other must concur. Negotiation is an optional provision (Schedule 5, Supplemental Provision 6). Negotiation and mediation are voluntary processes which depend on the co-operation of the parties, and either may lead to a binding result. If none of the options of negotiation, mediation or arbitration is used, or if either party is dissatisfied with the decision of an adjudicator, then the dispute will have to be resolved by arbitration or litigation.

10.2   There are therefore stages, either before or during the contract, where the parties have the opportunity to agree a preferred course of action. It is important for the contract administrator to understand and to be able to advise on these methods. In addition, the contract administrator ought to be familiar with the processes as they may find that they become involved in giving evidence. However, the contract administrator should be careful to avoid giving advice about the merits of a case, or how the employer should bring or defend a claim, as this is normally beyond the contract administrator's expertise, although, of course, some general advice and background information may be helpful.

10.3   The contract administrator should also tread carefully if the employer decides to attempt to resolve differences through negotiation. This might be the best solution to the problem, but the contract administrator has no authority to negotiate amendments to the terms of the contract or make ad hoc agreements on behalf of the employer. Even if the employer gives the contract administrator an extended authority to negotiate a settlement, where the dispute involves complex legal points, a lawyer would be the best choice to handle the negotiations.

Alternative dispute resolution

10.4   If negotiations fail to achieve an agreement, the parties may submit the dispute to 'alternative dispute resolution' (ADR), a term used to cover methods such as conciliation, mediation and the mini-trial. IC11 clause 9·1 requires each party to give serious consideration to a request by the other to use mediation. A footnote to clause 9·1 draws attention to the possibility of using mediation in clause 9·1, which refers to the Guide (IC/G). The Guide does not itself set out or advocate any particular procedure to be used in mediation; instead, it states that such choices are frequently better made by the parties when the dispute has actually arisen. The parties could, of course, supplement IC11 by selecting a mediator or mediator-appointing body and setting this out in their contract. As mediation is a consensual process, any reference to mediation would have to be supported by both parties.

10.5   Usually a mediator is appointed jointly by the parties, and will normally meet with the parties together and separately in an attempt to resolve the differences. The outcome is in the form of a recommendation which, if acceptable, can be signed as a legally binding agreement. This would then be enforceable in the same way as any other contract. However, if the recommendation is not acceptable to one of the parties and is not signed as a binding agreement, it cannot be imposed by law, and so the time spent on the mediation may appear to have been wasted.

10.6   Nevertheless, there can be many advantages to mediation. Unlike adjudication, arbitration or litigation, it is a non-adversarial process which tends to forge good relationships between the parties. Imposed solutions may leave at least one of the parties dissatisfied and may make it very difficult to work together in the future. If the parties are keen to promote a long-term business relationship they should give mediation serious consideration. Even if mediation does not result in a complete solution, it has been found in practice that it can help to clear the air on some of the issues involved and to establish common ground. This, in turn, might then pave the way for shorter and possibly less acrimonious arbitration or litigation.

Adjudication

10.7   The Housing Grants, Construction and Regeneration Act (HGCRA) 1996 Part II requires that parties to construction contracts falling within the definition set out in the Act have the right to refer any dispute to a process of adjudication which complies with requirements stipulated in the Act. Article 7 of IC11 restates this right, and refers to clause 9·2, which states that where a party decides to exercise this right 'the Scheme shall apply'. This refers to the Scheme for Construction Contracts, a piece of secondary legislation which sets out a procedure for the appointment of the adjudicator and the conduct of the adjudication. The Scheme takes effect as implied terms in a contract, if and to the extent that the parties have failed to agree on a procedure that complies with the Act.

10.8   By stating 'the Scheme shall apply', IC11 is effectively annexing the provisions of the Scheme to the form, which therefore become a binding part of the agreement between the parties. Clause 9·2, however, makes its application subject to certain conditions which relate to the appointment of the adjudicator.

10.9   Under IC11 the adjudicator may either be named in the contract particulars, or nominated by the nominating body identified in the contract particulars. It should be noted that the list of bodies has changed since IC05, and now includes, in addition to the RIBA, the RICS and the CIArb, the 'constructionadjudicators.com' and the Association of Independent Construction Adjudicators (AICA). A named adjudicator will normally enter into the JCT Adjudication Agreement (Named Adjudicator) (Adj/N) with the parties at the time the main contract is entered into.

10.10   The party wishing to refer a dispute to adjudication must first give notice under paragraph 1(1) of the Scheme. The notice may be issued at any time and should identify briefly the dispute or difference, give details of where and when it has arisen, set out the nature of the redress sought, and include the names and addresses of the parties, including any specified for the giving of notices (paragraph 1(3)). If no adjudicator is named, the parties may either agree an adjudicator or either party may apply to the 'nominator' identified in the contract particulars (paragraph 2(1)). If no nominator has been selected, then the contract states that the referring party may apply to any of the nominators listed in the contract particulars. The adjudicator will then send terms of appointment to the parties. In addition to the form for a named adjudicator, the JCT also publishes an Adjudication Agreement (Adj) for use in this situation.

10.11   The Scheme does not stipulate any qualifications in order to be an adjudicator, but does state that the adjudicator 'should be a natural person acting in his personal capacity' and should not be an employee of either of the parties (paragraph 4). In addition, IC11 requires that, where the dispute relates to clause 3·15 (repeat testing), the person appointed shall 'where practicable' be 'an individual with appropriate expertise in the specialist area or discipline relevant to the instruction or issue in dispute' (cl 9·2·2·1). Where the person does not have the appropriate expertise, that person must appoint an independent expert to advise and report.

10.12   The adjudicator is required to act impartially, must avoid incurring unnecessary expense (paragraph 12), and is not liable for anything done or omitted when acting properly as an adjudicator (paragraph 26).

10.13   The referring party must refer the dispute to the selected adjudicator within seven days of the date of the notice (paragraph 7(1)). The referral will normally include particulars of the dispute, and must include a copy of, or relevant extracts from, the contract, and any material it wishes the adjudicator to consider (paragraph 7(2)). A copy of the referral must be sent to the other party and the adjudicator must inform all parties of the date it was received (paragraph 7(3)).

10.14   The adjudicator will then set out the procedure to be followed. A preliminary meeting may be held to discuss this, otherwise the adjudicator may send the procedure and timetable to both parties. The party which did not initiate the adjudication (the responding party) will be required to respond by a stipulated deadline. The adjudicator is likely to hold a short hearing of a few days at which the parties can put forward further arguments and evidence. There may also be a site visit. Occasionally it may be possible to carry out the whole process by correspondence (often termed 'documents only').

10.15   The adjudicator is given considerable powers under the Scheme (e.g. paragraphs 13 and 20), including the right to take the initiative in obtaining the facts and the law, the right to issue directions, the right to revise decisions and certificates of the contract administrator, the right to carry out tests (subject to obtaining necessary consents), and the right to obtain from others necessary information and advice. The adjudicator must give advance notice if intending to take legal or technical advice.

10.16   The HGCRA 1996 requires that the decision is reached within 28 days of referral, but it does not state how this date is to be established (section 108(2)(c)). Under the Scheme, the 28 days start to run from the date of receipt of the referral notice (paragraph 19(1)).

The period can be extended by up to 14 days by the referring party, and further by agreement between the parties. The decision must be delivered forthwith to the parties, and the adjudicator may not retain it pending payment of the fee. The provisions state that the adjudicator must give reasons for the decision if requested to do so by the parties (paragraph 22).

10.17   The parties must meet their own costs of the adjudication, unless they have agreed that the adjudicator shall have the power to award costs. Under the Act, any agreement is ineffective unless it complies with section 108A, including that it is made in writing after a notice of adjudication is issued (SBC11 therefore does not contain such an agreement). The adjudicator, however, is entitled to charge fees and expenses (subject to any agreement to the contrary), although expenses are limited to those 'reasonably incurred' (paragraph 25). The adjudicator may apportion those fees between the parties, and the parties are jointly and severally liable to the adjudicator for any sum which remains outstanding following the adjudicator's determination. This means that in the event of default by one party, the other party becomes liable to the adjudicator for the outstanding amount.

10.18   The adjudicator's decision will be final and binding on the parties 'until the dispute is finally determined by legal proceedings, by arbitration, or by agreement between the parties'. The effect of this is that if either party is dissatisfied with the decision, it may raise the dispute again in arbitration or litigation as indicated in the contract particulars, or it may negotiate a fresh agreement with the other party. In all cases, however, the parties remain bound by the decision and must comply with it until the final outcome is determined.

10.19   If either party refuses to comply with the decision, the other may seek to enforce it through the courts. Generally, actions regarding adjudicators' decisions have been dealt with promptly by the courts and the recalcitrant party has been required to comply. Paragraph 22A of the Scheme allows the adjudicator to correct clerical or typographical errors in the decision, within five days of it being issued, either on the adjudicator's own initiative or because the parties have requested it, but this would not extend to reconsidering the substance of the dispute.

Arbitration

10.20   Arbitration refers to proceedings in which the arbitrator has power derived from a written agreement between the parties to a contract, and which is subject to the provisions of the Arbitration Act 1996. Arbitration awards are enforceable at law. An arbitrator's award can be subject to appeal on limited grounds.

10.21   If arbitration is preferred to litigation as the method for final determination of disputes, then this is confirmed by selecting Article 8 in the contract particulars (if no selection is made, then litigation will apply). The arbitration provisions are set out in clauses 9·3 to 9·8, which refer to the Construction Industry Model Arbitration Rules ('the Rules'). The Arbitration Act 1996 confers wide powers on the arbitrator unless the parties have agreed otherwise, but leaves detailed procedural matters to be agreed between the parties or, if not so agreed, to be decided by the arbitrator. To avoid problems arising, it is advisable to agree as much as possible of the procedural matters in advance, and IC11 does this by incorporating the Rules, which are very clearly written and self-explanatory. The specific edition referred to is the 2011 edition published by the JCT, which incorporates supplementary and advisory procedures, some of which are mandatory (Part A) and some of which apply only if agreed after the arbitration is begun (Part B). The paragraphs below refer to the JCT edition.

10.22   The party wishing to refer the dispute to arbitration must give notice as required by IC11 clause 9·4·1 and Rule 2.1, identifying briefly the dispute and requiring the party to agree to the appointment of an arbitrator. If the parties fail to agree within 14 days, either party may apply to the 'appointor', selected in advance from a list of organisations set out in the contract particulars. If no appointor is selected, then the contract states that the appointor will be the president or a vice-president of the RIBA. Under Rule 2.5 the arbitrator's appointment takes effect when he or she agrees to act, and is not subject to first reaching agreement with the parties on matters such as fees.

10.23   The arbitrator has the right and the duty to decide all procedural matters, subject to the parties' right to agree any matter (Rule 5.1). Within 14 days of appointment the parties must each send the arbitrator and each other a note indicating the nature of the dispute and amounts in issue, the estimated length for the hearing, if necessary, and the procedures to be followed (Rule 6.2). The arbitrator must hold a preliminary meeting within 21 days of appointment to discuss these matters (Rule 6.3). The first decision to make is whether Rule 7 (short hearing), Rule 8 (documents only) or Rule 9 (full procedure) is to apply. The decision will depend on the scale and type of dispute.

10.24   Under all three Rules referred to above, the parties exchange statements of claim and of defence, together with copies of documents and witness statements on which they intend to rely. Under Rule 8, the arbitrator makes the award based on the documentary evidence only. Under Rule 9, the arbitrator will hold a hearing at which the parties or their representatives can put forward further arguments and evidence. There may also be a site visit. The JCT Amendments set out time limits for these procedures.

10.25   Under Rule 7 a hearing is to be held within 21 days of the date when Rule 7 becomes applicable, and the parties must exchange documents not later than seven days prior to the hearing. The hearing should last no longer than one day. The arbitrator publishes the award within one month of the hearing. The parties bear their own costs.

10.26   The arbitrator is given a wide range of powers under Rule 4, including:

•   the power to obtain advice (Rule 4.2);

•   the powers set out in section 38 of the Arbitration Act 1996 (Rule 4.3);

•   the power to order the preservation of work, goods and materials even though they are a part of work that is continuing (Rule 4.4);

- the power to request the parties to carry out tests (Rule 4.5); and

- the power to award costs (Rule 4.6).

10.27   Under clause 9·5 of IC11 the arbitrator is also given wide powers to review and revise any certificate, opinion, decision, requirement or notice and to disregard them if need be, where seeking to determine all matters in dispute.

10.28   Where the arbitrator has the power to award costs, this will normally be done on a judicial basis, i.e. the loser will pay the winner's costs (Rule 13.1). The arbitrator will be entitled to charge fees and expenses and will apportion those fees between the parties on the same basis. The parties are jointly and severally liable to the arbitrator for fees and expenses incurred.

Arbitration and adjudication

10.29   Under Article 8 any dispute that has been referred to an adjudicator may be referred to arbitration if this is required by either party. Clause 1·9·3 states that, even where the decision has been given after the final certificate is issued, either party may refer the dispute to arbitration, provided the arbitration is commenced within 28 days of the adjudicator's decision. It is not entirely clear, however, whether this will affect the date at which the final certificate will become conclusive evidence of the matters listed under clause 1·9·1, which may, of course, have been the matters disputed under the adjudication.

Arbitration or litigation

10.30   As stated above, IC11 contains alternative provisions for arbitration and litigation in Articles 8 and 9, and a choice has to be made before tender documents are sent out. Both processes give rise to binding and enforceable decisions. Both tend to be lengthy and expensive, although there are provisions for short forms of arbitration.

10.31   Litigation cases involving claims for amounts greater than £25,000 are normally heard in the High Court, and construction cases are usually heard in the Technology and Construction Court, a specialist department of the High Court which deals with technical or scientific cases. Procedures in court follow the Civil Procedure Rules, with the timetable and other detailed arrangements being determined by the court. A judge will hear the case and although, in the past, parties were required to be represented by barristers, now they may represent themselves, or elect to be represented by an 'advisor'.

10.32   Disputes in building contracts have traditionally been settled by arbitration. Arbitrators are usually senior and experienced members of one of the construction professions, and for many years it was felt that they had a greater understanding of construction projects and the disputes that arise, than might be found in the courts. These days, however, the judges of the Technology and Construction Court have extensive experience of technical construction disputes. The high standards now evident in these courts are likely to be matched in practice by only a few arbitrators.

10.33   The court has powers to order that actions regarding related matters are joined (for example, where disputes between an employer and contractor, and contractor and sub-contractor, concern the same issues). This is more difficult to achieve in arbitration. Even if all parties have agreed to the Construction Industry Model Arbitration Rules, the appointing bodies must have been alerted and have agreed to appoint the same arbitrator (Rules 2.6 and 2.7). If the same arbitrator is appointed, he or she may order concurrent hearings (Rule 3.7), but may only order consolidated proceedings with the consent of all the parties (Rule 3.9), which is often difficult to obtain. The court's powers may therefore offer an advantage in multi-party disputes, by avoiding duplication of hearings and possible conflicting outcomes.

10.34   There remain, however, two key advantages to using arbitration. The first is that in arbitration the proceedings can be kept private, which is usually of paramount importance to construction professionals and companies, and is often a deciding factor in selecting arbitration. In court, the proceedings are open to the public and the press, and the judgment is published and widely available.

10.35   The second advantage to the parties is that the arbitration process is consensual. The parties are free to agree on timing, place, representation and the individual arbitrator. This autonomy carries with it the benefits of increased convenience, and possible savings in time and expense. The parties avoid having to wait their turn at the High Court, and may choose a time and place for the hearing which is convenient to all. In arbitration, however, the parties have to pay the arbitrator and meet the cost of renting the premises in which the hearing is held.

10.36   It should perhaps be noted that, even where parties have selected arbitration under Article 8, it is still open for them to select litigation once a dispute develops. If, however, one party commences court proceedings, the other may ask the court to stay the proceedings on the grounds that an arbitration agreement already exists. This would not apply to litigation to enforce an adjudicator's decision, as Article 8 excludes all disputes regarding the enforcement of a decision of an adjudicator from the jurisdiction of the arbitrator. If, on the other hand, the parties had originally selected litigation, this would not prevent them from subsequently agreeing to take a dispute to arbitration, but in such cases they would also have to agree how the arbitrator is to be appointed and which procedural rules are to apply.

References

Publications

Aeberli, P. *Focus on Construction Contract Formation,* RIBA Publishing, London (2003)

Chappell, D. *The JCT Intermediate Building Contracts 2005,* Blackwell Publishing, Oxford (2006)

Chappell, D. *IC11 Contract Administration Guide,* RIBA Publishing, London (2011)

Furst, S. and Ramsey, V. (eds) *Keating on Construction Contracts.* Sweet & Maxwell, London (2006)

Hyams, D. *Construction Companion to Briefing,* RIBA Publications, London (2001).

JCT/BDP. *JCT Guide to the Use of Performance Specifications,* RIBA Publications, London (2001).

Cases

(Note that full reports of the majority of cases can now be found on the internet, for example at http://www.bailii.org/ew/cases/EWHC/TCC/)

Alexander and another v Mercouris [1979] 1 WLR 1270	3.14
Alfred McAlpine Capital Projects Ltd v Tilebox Ltd [2005] BLR 271	4.44
Alfred McAlpine Homes North Ltd v Property and Land Contractors Ltd (1995) 76 BLR 59	6.21
Archivent Sales & Developments Ltd v Strathclyde Regional Council (1984) 27 BLR 98 (Court of Session, Outer House)	7.16, 7.19
Balfour Beatty Building Ltd v Chestermont Properties Ltd (1993) 62 BLR 1	4.21
Bath and North East Somerset District Council v Mowlem plc [2004] BLR 153 (CA)	5.41
British Telecommunications plc v James Thompson & Sons (Engineers) Ltd [1999] BLR 35 (HL)	8.10
City Inn Ltd v Shepherd Construction Ltd [2008] CILL 2537, Outer House Court of Session	4.28
Colbart Ltd v H Kumar (1992) 59 BLR 89	7.51
Construction Partnership UK Ltd v Leek Developments Ltd [2006] CILL 2357 TCC	9.8
Co-operative Insurance Society v Henry Boot Scotland and others (2002) 84 Con LR 164	3.6
Croudace Ltd v The London Borough of Lambeth (1986) 33 BLR 20 (CA)	6.25
Crown Estates Commissioners v John Mowlem & Co. Ltd (1994) 70 BLR 1 (CA)	7.51
Dawber Williamson Roofing Ltd v Humberside County Council (1979) 14 BLR 70	7.19
Department of Environment for Northern Ireland v Farrans (Construction) Ltd (1982) 19 BLR 1 (NI)	4.48
Dhamija and another v Sunningdale Joineries Ltd and others [2010] EWHC 2396 (TCC)	7.13
Domsalla v Dyason [2007] BLR 348	1.13
F G Minter Ltd v Welsh Health Technical Services Organisation (1980) 13 BLR 1 (CA)	6.21
Ferson Contractors Ltd v Levolux AT Ltd [2003] BLR 118	9.19
Glenlion Construction Ltd v The Guinness Trust (1987) 39 BLR 89	4.11
Greater London Council v Cleveland Bridge and Engineering Co. (1986) 34 BLR 50 (CA)	4.9
Henry Boot Construction Ltd v Alstom Combined Cycles [2000] BLR 247	6.13
Henry Boot Construction (UK) Ltd v Malmaison Hotel (Manchester) Ltd (1999) 70 Con LR 32 (TCC)	4.28
H Fairweather & Co. Ltd v London Borough of Wandsworth (1987) 39 BLR 106	4.27
H W Nevill (Sunblest) Ltd v William Press & Son Ltd (1981) 20 BLR 78	4.37
Holland Hannen & Cubitts (Northern) Ltd v Welsh Health Technical Services Organisation (1985) 35 BLR 1 (CA)	5.41
Impresa Castelli SpA v Cola Holdings Ltd (2002) CLJ 45	4.34
J F Finnegan Ltd v Community Housing Association Ltd (1993) 65 BLR 103	4.48
J F Finnegan Ltd v Community Housing Association Ltd (1995) 77 BLR 22 (CA)	4.46

Clause Index *by paragraph number*

Subject Index *by paragraph number*